D0906429

455.4
BOL

A-863

NVENT

RY

GOOD SHEPHERD CONVENT
ST. LOUIS
PROVINCIAL LIBRARY

THE MONOGRAPH SERIES OF
THE PSYCHOANALYTIC STUDY OF THE CHILD

Monograph No. 1

THE HAMPSTEAD PSYCHOANALYTIC INDEX

*A Study of the Psychoanalytic Case Material
of a Two-year-old Child*

THE PSYCHOANALYTIC STUDY OF THE CHILD
MONOGRAPH NO. 1

The Hampstead Psychoanalytic Index

*A Study of the Psychoanalytic Case Material
of a Two-year-old Child*

By
JOHN BOLLAND, M.B., Ch.B.
and
JOSEPH SANDLER, M.A., Ph.D., D.Sc.

in collaboration with MARIA KAWENOKA,
LILY NEURATH, HANNA ENGL KENNEDY,
AGNES BENE, SHEILA BAKER

155.4
B OL

The Hampstead Child-Therapy Clinic, London

GOOD SHEPHERD CONVENT
ST. LOUIS
PROVINCIAL LIBRARY

INTERNATIONAL UNIVERSITIES PRESS, INC.
NEW YORK

GOOD SHEPHERD CONVENT
ST. LOUIS
PROVINCIAL LIBRARY

THE MONOGRAPH SERIES OF
THE PSYCHOANALYTIC STUDY OF THE CHILD

Managing Editors

Ruth S. Eissler, M.D.   Heinz Hartmann, M.D.
Anna Freud, LL.D., Sc.D.   Marianne Kris, M.D.

Editorial Assistant

Lottie M. Newman

Copyright 1965, by International Universities Press, Inc.

Library of Congress Catalog Card Number: 65-23575

Manufactured in the United States of America

THE MONOGRAPH SERIES OF
THE PSYCHOANALYTIC STUDY OF THE CHILD

has been established to make possible the publication of papers on psychoanalytic research which, due to their length, cannot be included in the annual volumes of *The Psychoanalytic Study of the Child*.

All contributions for publication in the Monograph Series will be by invitation only. The Editors regret that they do not have facilities to read unsolicited manuscripts.

The first monographs will deal with various phases of the research work done at the Hampstead Child-Therapy Course and Clinic in London by Anna Freud and her collaborators.

The Editors

To Anna Freud and Dorothy Burlingham

PREFACE

As a sample of work done in the Hampstead Child-Therapy Clinic, the case of Andy has a variety of purposes.

As a clinical example it illustrates successful analytic treatment carried out in the case of a very young boy who suffered from developmental upsets and made his environment suffer through his aggressive outbursts, his disturbances of sleep, and his difficult behavior. Analysis in his case is shown to have proved therapeutic with regard to early symptom formation and truly preventive so far as the threat of a later full-blown infantile neurosis was concerned.

There are various ways in which the mother of a two-and-a-half-year-old participates in plans for his treatment: it can take the form of simultaneous analysis of mother and child; or of treatment of the child through the mother (guided by the analyst); or of straightforward child analysis with added guidance of the mother. What was chosen in Andy's case was the third possibility, but with "mother guidance" given in a special form. Without undergoing analysis or any form of psychotherapy herself, Andy's mother was included in the analytic process, shared in her son's involvement with transference and resistance, as well as in his receiving and working through of interpretation and enlightenment. At the end of treatment, both mother and child could be seen to emerge together on a new level of understanding, liberation and development. The consecutive steps of this satisfying venture

are illustrated in detail by the weekly reports which form
Chapter 5 of the Monograph.

For the rest, Andy's case is used to demonstrate the "indexing" of analytic material, which is one of the ways in
which analysts may learn to lay down their personal clinical
impressions to be shared with others. How this is being done
in the Hampstead Clinic is explained at length in Chapter 1.
What we hope to construct by this laborious method is something of a "collective analytic memory," i.e., a storehouse of
analytic material which places at the disposal of the single
thinker and author an abundance of facts gathered by many,
thereby transcending the narrow confines of individual experience and extending the possibilities for insightful study,
for constructive comparisons between cases, for deductions
and generalizations, and finally for extrapolations of theory
from clinical therapeutic work.

                                                    Anna Freud
London, March 1965

CONTENTS

ACKNOWLEDGMENTS

This investigation was supported (in part) by Public Health Service Research Grant No. M-5683, MH (1) from the National Institute of Mental Health, Bethesda, Maryland; and by a joint grant from the Foundations' Fund for Research in Psychiatry, New Haven, Connecticut, and the Psychoanalytic Research and Development Fund, Inc., New York.

The material used has been collected at the Hampstead Child-Therapy Clinic, a therapeutic and research center financed by the following foundations: The Field Foundation, Inc., New York; The Anna Freud Foundation, New York; The Estate of Flora Haas, New York; The Old Dominion Foundation, U.S.A.; The Psychoanalytic Research and Development Fund, Inc., New York; and the National Institute of Mental Health, Bethesda, Maryland.

The authors owe a debt to Miss Anna Freud and Mrs. Dorothy Burlingham for their constant encouragement. Thanks are due to all those who have been associated with the work of the Index since its inception; to Miss Margaret Bavin who supervised Andy's treatment; and, not least, to Andy himself.

THE MONOGRAPH SERIES OF
THE PSYCHOANALYTIC STUDY OF THE CHILD

Monograph No. 1

THE HAMPSTEAD PSYCHOANALYTIC INDEX

A Study of the Psychoanalytic Case Material
of a Two-year-old Child

CHAPTER 1

INTRODUCTION

This monograph presents an account of a single case of a
very young child who has been treated psychoanalytically at
the Hampstead Child-Therapy Clinic, London; but its primary aim is not that of case presentation. Andy's clinical and
psychoanalytic material was subjected to the process known
as *indexing*, the aims and methods of which are described in
Part II. The purpose of this monograph is to demonstrate,
with Andy's material, just how the Hampstead Psychoanalytic Index can be applied, and the value of this procedure
for research in psychoanalysis.

The Hampstead Index project was begun over ten years
ago. In a number of previous studies attempts have been
made to solve some of the theoretical and practical problems
which have arisen in the course of the work of indexing.[1]
These reports have been mainly concerned with specific problems, and the present work aims at supplementing these with
an account of the indexing of a single case.

One of the duties of psychoanalytic child therapists and
analysts who have cases in daily analysis at the Hampstead
Clinic is documentation, for the psychoanalytic material col-

[1] See Sandler (1960, 1962a, 1962b), Sandler and Rosenblatt (1962); Sandler,
Kawenoka, Neurath, Rosenblatt, Schnurmann, and Sigal (1962); Sandler and
Nagera (1963); Sandler, Holder, and Meers (1963); Sandler and Joffe (1964a,
1964b, 1965), Joffe and Sandler (1965).

1

lected there is the property of the Clinic as a whole, and is meant to be available for research. A weekly report has to be written for each case, sufficient to give the important features of the week's work; in addition, a further and rather more comprehensive report is composed several times a year.

As more and more cases have been treated, the quantity of recorded reports has grown, and the Clinic was, some years ago, faced with the problem of making use of all of this material for the purposes of research. It became apparent that the accumulation of records, however accurate and illuminating, did not in itself constitute research.

Two real problems had to be faced; problems which could in time become acute. The first of these was that of finding the best way of making this material available to research workers, and the second that of providing the therapists themselves with the very necessary feeling that their efforts in preparing these reports were not wasted. It was clearly essential for the Clinic to find some sort of feedback of achievement for the therapists who had spent so many hours working at their cases for the records. A solution to these problems was suggested by Mrs. Dorothy Burlingham, in the form of a proposed Index to the Hampstead case material. The Index project, as it was originally conceived, had two major aims: the first was to make the Clinic's vast amount of analytic material more readily accessible for research, and also for teaching and reference purposes, while the second aim was to open up new lines of research by assembling analytic data in such a way as to facilitate comparison among cases.

The Index was to be constructed on the same basis as an index to a book might be assembled,[2] but in devising a scheme of classification it was felt to be essential that the uniqueness and individuality of each case be preserved, while

2 Although this was our original intention, it soon became clear that we were going to have something on our hands which was vastly different from an ordinary book index.

being at the same time comprehended within a common theoretical framework.

A description of the Index and some of the procedures involved in indexing a case is given in Part II. These procedures have been evolved during the course of a pilot study in which therapists, together with an Index working party, classified the analytic and other relevant material of fifty cases which were in daily analysis. From this preliminary work it was possible to construct a set of common categories and an indexing procedure which was aimed at retaining the flexibility of therapists' reports, but which at the same time would provide a comprehensive system of classification. The material drawn on from the Index consists of all the therapist knows about the child, and considers to be of importance and interest in the case. Most of this is on record in the Social History and in the Weekly and other reports on the case.

This material can be classified under two main headings. The first, the *General Case Material,* contains information of a factual or psychological nature referring to the external reality of the child (for example, parental attitudes, family history, illnesses, etc.). The second, and by far the greatest division in the Index, contains the *Psychoanalytic Material.* Each division is further subdivided into a number of clinically or psychologically meaningful sections and subsections. Thus the information in the Social History of a case can be classified under a number of subheadings such as *Background* and *Biographical Data,* and the psychoanalytic material is ordered under the various subheadings of the sections: Object relationships, Instinctual material, Fantasies, Ego (Defenses), other Ego material, Superego, Symptoms, and Treatment Situation and Technique.

For each child we have two identical sets of typed cards. On each card is typed the name of the child, and his age at the beginning of daily treatment. Following this there is a subject heading, the age of the child at the time of indexing, and brief text references to the relevant pages of the case notes. These references indicate where in the case reports fuller details on the subject given in the heading on the card may be found and the text on the card abstracts the material to be found there.

One of the sets of cards is called the *Case Index* and is filed according to the name of the child. The complete set of cards represents an abstract of the family background, developmental and social history, and especially the psychopathology and analytic treatment of the child. The other set, like the subject catalogue in a library, is distributed under the various headings of the *Subject Index*. Under any given subject heading will appear the cards of all the cases in which therapists have recorded material relevant to that heading; thus the Case Index facilitates intracase studies, whereas the Subject Index facilitates intercase research.

Because of the multiple and overdetermination of analytic material, provision has had to be made for the classification of any unit of psychoanalytic observation from a number of different points of view. In order to deal with this a cross-referencing system was devised in an attempt to permit the integration of the various viewpoints, while aiming at the same time not to detract from their individual significance.[3] Thus, for example, an item of transference behavior indicating oral dependence may be traced through its dynamic aspect (oral libidinal and aggressive aims); or through its ego and superego aspects; or through its relevance to the course of psychosexual development; or through the form in which it appears in object relations both within the transference and elsewhere. The system of cross-reference cards is designed to help those seeking to find such a piece of case material to approach it from any one of a number of different conceptual paths.

In order to preserve the individual flavor of a case, as well as to reflect the differences between therapists in their approach

[3] In the case of Andy cross-references have been omitted in the interest of simplicity.

to cases, the therapist is encouraged to order and classify the material according to those categories which he or she considers most satisfactory. For each therapist there is an Index adviser (and a committee to advise the adviser), and in joint consultation the initial classification is extended by cross-referencing to other relevant headings. In this way the initiative of the therapist and his own classifying habits are retained, yet the case material can be placed within the same multidimensional system of classification that is used by other therapists and for other cases.

As treatment progresses, more information becomes available. Changes occur in the therapist's understanding of the case and changes occur in the patient. To include this additional material, the case is reindexed annually for the duration of treatment. Subsequent information is added to the earlier information, and the development of the material in the course of the analysis can be followed. (In the case of Andy, a second indexing was performed, and the text indicates which material was added at the second indexing.)

An essential part of the Index project has been the construction of a number of Index Manuals to help the therapists in their indexing. These manuals, which undergo continual revision, do not lay down a formal set of headings. If a therapist feels that he or she would like to invent a new heading, or to classify the material of a case in a rather different way, this is perfectly permissible, if the therapist can make out a case for it. The manuals explain, in more or less detail as required, what kind of material is to be indexed in each section. They also define the use of terms for the purpose of the Index. The manuals are used for teaching purposes in connection with material from the Index and are designed to help the research worker to orientate himself in the Index.

The Subject Index is not a scheme prepared on purely theoretical considerations, but is continually being revised on the basis of the clinical material gathered in the course of child analyses, material which is then classified in accordance with our analytic theory. The various research projects also have the secondary effect of causing new headings to appear, and the diagnostic research, making use of the Developmental Profile devised by Anna Freud (1965), has in particular stimulated a number of changes in the manuals.

References will be found in the descriptions which follow to permanent cross-reference cards (Guide Cards). These represent sets of links between various headings in the Index which apply to all cases.

In the Case indexing of Andy in Part II, extracts from the manuals are presented under the appropriate headings. It should be stressed that *only the explanatory material which refers to the indexing of Andy* is given, and the explanations and definitions given represent *no more than a fraction of that contained in the Index manuals*. It is important that this be kept in mind in reading the pages which follow.

The Manuals are organized at present as follows:

1. General Case Material
2. Ego (General)
3. Ego (Anxiety)
4. Ego (Defenses)
5. Instinctual
6. Object Relationships
7. Fantasies
8. Superego
9. Symptoms
10. Treatment Situation and Technique

Andy was in psychoanalytic treatment with Dr. Bolland[4] from the age of two years and five months. He had 221 analytic sessions, and was three years and seven months of age when treatment ended. Although Andy's case is of intrinsic interest in that he was so young when treatment commenced

---

4 Under the supervision of Miss Margaret Bavin; Mrs. Maria Kawenoka acted as Index adviser and collaborated in the preparation of Andy's material for indexing.

and terminated, and because the detailed reports on his treatment offer an insight into the technical aspects of his treatment, we would reiterate that the main purpose of presenting his material in this monograph is to illustrate the indexing procedure. This procedure has been applied to about one hundred cases treated at the Clinic, and for each child indexed a unique set of index cards has been prepared. The headings applicable to Andy do not necessarily apply *in toto* to other indexed cases, and represent a selection of the much larger pool of headings (and their definitions) used for other cases.

Indexing a treated case is an exercise which we believe to be of the greatest value in integrating clinical material with psychoanalytic theory. And, as we hope the reader will agree, the process of indexing clinical observations is a stimulus to the clarification and amplification of the body of psychoanalytic theory itself.

Part I

**ANDY'S CLINICAL AND
PSYCHOANALYTIC MATERIAL**

CHAPTER 2

A CLINICAL NOTE ON ANDY

Andy was two years and five months old when treatment started. He had been referred to the Hampstead Child-Therapy Clinic because of his mother's anxiety about his symptoms. He would not go to sleep until very late and always awoke during the night, when he came into his parents' bed, which was in the same room as his own. He would become overexcited and overactive in the presence of other children, and his mother feared that he would wear himself out. She said that she had always been anxious about him, particularly because of his previous physical illnesses. More recently she had felt very guilty about her ambivalence toward him—she was often irritated by him and would smack him, immediately feeling remorseful and remembering his "bad start in life."

This "bad start" was due to gastroenteritis, for which he had been admitted to a hospital at the age of three weeks. He was very ill and drip-feeding had had to be instituted. He remained in the hospital until he was four months old—and during his stay there, contact with his mother was minimal. Thereafter he was hospitalized twice more; once for bronchitis at the age of eight months for two days (on this occasion he was admitted only because his mother was admitted to another ward with a broken arm); on the second occasion, at the age of eighteen months, he was admitted for twenty-

11

four hours for observation, following a convulsion associated with pyrexia. He had another such convulsion at about his second birthday, but was not hospitalized on that occasion.

The parents were young working-class people of obvious sincerity. They were proud of their pugnacious little boy and keen for help. They also had neurotic problems—the mother had some hysterical symptoms, including acrophobia and a fear of being on the streets after dark; the father was immature and tied to his parents, in whose house the little family lived. The paternal grandparents seemed also to be disturbed, particularly the grandfather, but it seemed that Andy was a much-loved child, the grandparents doting on him and indulging him considerably.

Intensive treatment was recommended and eagerly accepted by the parents.

Treatment was on the basis of five fifty-minute sessions a week. For the first two weeks Andy and his mother came together to the treatment room and thereafter Andy came alone while his mother stayed in the waiting room. His mother came to see the analyst once a week. From the very beginning, the mother showed an all-too-rare capacity to use her sessions in a way fruitful for the treatment and for her relationship with the child. An unsophisticated and uneducated woman, she showed much common sense and empathy with Andy. This use of her sessions was facilitated by what the analyst considered to be a positive transference from an idealized father. Sessions with her consisted of her bringing news of Andy's doings at home, family developments, and her feelings; the analyst gave reassurance, advice, and, very rarely, interpretations. It had been hoped that the father would also be seen frequently, but he avoided this by one means or another until the last few weeks of treatment when he came to see the analyst once a fortnight. These sessions also seemed helpful.

Treatment sessions with Andy were always lively. He showed very early an unusual capacity for verbalization. At

first this was accompanied by action—aggressive and affec-
tionate; later, verbalization of affect and thoughts predominated by far over action. His verbal capacity was probably
fostered by his living with four adults, and indeed his vocabu-
lary of swearwords could have been considered adequate for
any bargee. The relationship with the analyst was soon established and remained constant throughout treatment—he
regarded the analyst as his friend (and always called him by
that name), but a friend who could be sworn at. This relationship was maintained despite the vicissitudes of the transference.

From the indexed material, it might appear that Andy's
difficulties were not such as warranted intensive treatment,
and indeed the course of the analysis suggests that the progressive and maturational processes would have carried him
through the developmental stages fairly successfully without
treatment. Nevertheless, the analyst felt that the child was
in danger of developing a very strong fixation at the anal-
sadistic stage, which was dominant at the time of referral,
and that the symptoms themselves could neither be considered as transitory nor be handled by guidance of the mother
alone.

It is hoped that the course of treatment can be seen in the
Weekly Reports and indexing. The outcome of treatment, as
seen and reported on at two recent follow-up sessions with
Andy and his mother, seems to be satisfactory. Andy made a
successful entry into nursery school at the end of the intensive
phase of treatment, which lasted for thirteen months, and he
has now happily started at a junior school at the age of five.
His mother's reports indicate that latency features are already
present, particularly in his move out to the world of his age
peers. His symptoms do not now exist, although his teacher
reported to the mother that Andy, in a class of forty five-year-
olds, finds it difficult to sit still for more than half an hour
and does not always do what he is told! Perhaps two remarks
that Andy made to the analyst at the last follow-up interview

may be quoted without comment. When the analyst went into the waiting room, Andy rushed toward him with a smile, saying, "Look, friend, I've got a tie just like yours"; and on reaching the treatment room he considered the analyst and said, with some compassion, "You know, friend, *you* are getting old."

Andy was indexed first after eight months of treatment, and a second indexing was performed ten months after the first. Thus his age at the time of first indexing was three years one month and at second indexing three years eleven months.

The reports by the analyst during the course of treatment are given in full. It is hoped that these not only will give the reader an over-all and sequential picture of the treatment, but will also enable him to check the sources of reference for each Index card; the extracts quoted in the cards can then be seen within the context of the treatment situation.

These reports are mainly the Weekly Reports required of the analyst for each patient treated at the Hampstead Child-Therapy Clinic. Such reports are intended to be a summary of the events of the week's sessions, including interpretative work and responses to it, together with any formulation the analyst feels able to make at any particular stage of the treatment. In this case, the Weekly Reports are published as originally written, except for minor changes made for purposes of preserving confidentiality. It will be seen that they include errors in technique and misunderstandings of material, and no attempt has been made to rewrite the reports with hindsight. The analyst hopes that what was badly done by him in the treatment, as well as what he thinks was well done, will be useful to readers, especially to those who are undergoing training in child analysis and to their supervisors.

CHAPTER 3

AN INTERVIEW WITH MOTHER AND ANDY

This is an account of an interview conducted by Dr. Bolland for the purpose of combining the taking of a Social History with the making of a Diagnostic Assessment. Andy was aged two years and five months at the time of this interview.

Referral

Andy was referred by a child psychiatrist in a children's hospital who knew that I was looking for a child under the age of five as a training case. The problem, as given to this doctor, was Andy's general excitability and sleeping difficulty.

Mother

Mrs. V. is a young, healthy-looking woman of twenty-six. She is fairly tall, slender, with beautifully kept blond hair. Her eyes are of an unusual green color. During the interview she was flushed and near to tears at times. She impressed me by her honesty and sincerity. Her naïvety was refreshing, but she was not without insight. She was very anxious, but had obviously determined that she must tell me as straightforwardly as she could how she felt.

The Child

Andy has a striking resemblance to his mother, with blond hair, red cheeks, and green eyes. The difference in their facial expression was that instead of looking anxious, he looked slightly pugnacious. At first he kept very close to her and without his asking directly, she picked him up so that he could play with a toy motor car on the table while sitting on her knee. This was obviously what he wanted, and she did it quite naturally. After a short time he wanted to get down, and at the first sign of this she let him down to play. He played with the toys at a small table on the other side of the room from his mother and me, then he would take some of them to show her, and finally brought some to me—to tell me their names and get my praise for being so knowledgeable: "Duck-duck, horsie, choo-choo train, chair," and so on. He mostly used single words, but once or twice used simple sentences, such as "That's a chair" or "Make it ring" (about the toy telephone). At the end of the interview his mother told him to leave the toy he was playing with and offered him his own toy train. He was obviously reluctant to accept this at first and the struggle could be quite clearly seen, but after a few moments of silent hesitation, he complied and departed with a spontaneous "Bye-bye."

The Problem

Mrs. V. put the problem immediately in terms of her own difficulty in tolerating Andy's restlessness, his not going to sleep at the "proper time" (7 to 7:30 P.M.) and his waking during the night. From the beginning it was a question of her asking for help for both of them—for Andy so that he did not wear himself out so much, and for herself so that she should not make things even worse for him than they were. She feels very guilty about being so angry with him sometimes that she is driven to smacking him; she knows this is not the way to handle him, but feels that she cannot stop herself when the situation goes beyond a certain point. She thinks he is very aggressive toward other children, but not to all; e.g., he has a special friend of the same age who is "exactly the opposite" of Andy—he is quiet and gentle, yet they get on very well together and Andy has never been known to hit his friend.

She thinks that the fact that they are living with her husband's parents aggravates her difficulty with Andy. She does not like her mother-in-law, and when she was first married she could not bear to stay in the house alone with her. She can do this now, but feels that her mother-in-law is very critical. She gets all sorts of conflicting advice from her own family and from her in-laws and this confuses her. However, she and her husband are hoping to get a flat of their own in about six months, and then she will feel free to bring Andy up in her own way. "Everybody has their own way and I think *her* way is wrong, but I'm not exactly in a position to tell her so if I'm living in her house. She thinks I'm stupid to worry about Andy, that he'll grow out of it—I don't think that is true, and anyway, I wouldn't like to take a chance on it, if there's anything that can be done *now*."

Development

Mrs. V. thinks that Andy had a bad start in life and that his early ill-health may tell against him later on. He was born in a maternity hospital and was 7 pounds at birth. He was breast-fed, but this did not last for long. They left the hospital when he was ten days old and during the first week after leaving the hospital he gained half a pound. However, the next week he lost this and was off his food. She took him to see her doctor, who arranged his admission to a hospital for gastroenteritis. Andy was in the hospital from the age of three weeks to four months. At eight months he was admitted again to a hospital with bronchitis. Mrs. V. thinks that he would not have been admitted on this occasion if it had not been that she herself had fallen off a stepladder and broken her arm and *she* was admitted for two days. He was again hospitalized for two days at the age of one year, for observation following a convulsion which was associated with a cold and a very high temperature.

He had another such convulsion with similar symptoms close to his second birthday, but was not admitted on that occasion. Her doctor told her that it was the high temperature which had caused the convulsion and that such things were fairly common in young children. Andy has been perfectly well since then, but Mrs. V. gets very worried about his pallor when he is very tired.

Breast feeding naturally stopped when he was admitted to the hospital on the first occasion, and there have been no feeding difficulties to speak of.

Teething was unremarkable. She expected to have sleepless nights during this, and got them.

Walking started at about one year, and he had three or four words at eighteen months.

She started toilet training him at seven months and he was a "good boy," being dry and clean at the age of sixteen to eighteen months. However, this did not last long, although he has remained clean—he always asks for his potty in good time—but for the last two months he has been a bit late when asking when he wants to urinate, with the result that he often has a wet patch on his trousers. When I said that she might have been a bit too optimistic in expecting him to be clean and dry at that age, she said, "Do you think so?" with relief in her voice.

He has always been very active in his play, not to say destructive. His parents bought him a puppy for his second birthday, but he and the puppy were always "quarreling" (as if they were both children) and the mother-in-law kicked up such a fuss that they gave the dog away. She and Andy went on a week's holiday and when they came back the dog had gone. He has never mentioned this pup until a week ago when she heard him "talking to himself," saying, "Where have you been, Rover—did you go down the road?" She and her husband have now decided that he should have another puppy, preferably a smaller one than the last, and Mr. V. is going to fix it with his mother. They decided on this because he is always talking about another dog in the neighboring house.

Domestic Arrangements

The parents and Andy have only one room of their own, in which all three sleep. The mother recognizes how unsatisfactory this is, and cites Andy's having a bedroom of his own as one of their urgent needs.

Mother's Personal History

She was the youngest of five children. Her mother died when she was eighteen months old, and she spent the next year moving round from one family to another until finally she found a home with her second-eldest sister. I commented on the fact that her own early history might have led to her conviction that children do not "grow out of" early difficulties. She said she is sure of it. Her sexual life with her husband has never really been very satisfactory. She and her husband talk about it, trying to find an explanation for the difficulties and a way to improve it. They came to the conclusion once that it probably had something to do with a very frightening experience she had had when she was five. A boy cousin aged ten had locked her in a cupboard and she was very frightened, thinking she would suffocate.

She worked as a shop assistant and continued work after she married until just before Andy's birth. Recently she took a part-time job which would allow her to take Andy with her, but he was so unhappy about this that she gave it up after three weeks. She had been trying to earn some extra money to save for the time when they would get a home of their own.

Father's Personal History

Mrs. V. said little about this, except that he is the same age as she (twenty-six), works as a laborer, and has several brothers and sisters. He brought her to the Clinic today, but could not wait. She says he is just as keen for help as she is.

Treatment Arrangements

I told Andy's mother about the diagnostic procedure, adding that there was some doubt in my mind whether, if treatment were recommended (it would mean their coming to the Clinic five times a week), she would be able to manage the journey. She told me that there is a more or less direct bus route from home to the Clinic, but even if the journey were more difficult, she would do it. She wants help badly, has no other child, has little or nothing to do during the day, and would be glad to get away from her mother-in-law every day for an hour or two.

I made a point of telling her that if treatment were recommended and she accepted it, she would be present with Andy and the therapist, at least at the beginning, because, as she herself realized, she was very much part of the whole situation and would want to learn about Andy and herself for the other twenty-three hours of the day. I wanted specially to emphasize this because of her own history and the fear which she might have of having her child stolen from her.

Comments

Andy's problem has largely to do with his aggression and his task in this is made immeasurably more difficult than usual because of the very early separation and the present domestic arrangements, by which he sleeps in the same room as the parents.

Similarly, Mrs. V.'s problems about her ambivalence toward Andy and her doubts about her ability to bring up her first child successfully are exaggerated by the external circumstances. It may be, of course, that these adverse circumstances are not fully struggled against because of their being a kind of need for repetition associated with her history, in which the hated mother-in-law may represent the mother who left her by dying.

Nevertheless, there is a very keenly felt need for help for herself as well as for her child, and I think this could be a very worth-while analytic case, with a lot of work being done with the mother.

CHAPTER 4

AN INTERVIEW WITH MOTHER, FATHER, AND ANDY

As Mr. V. was on night shift this week, he was fortunately able to come to this interview, which was for the purpose of offering analysis to Andy, and to discuss the practical details involved. I had hoped the father would be able to come, as I wanted a meeting between us before treatment actually started.

Mr. V. is the same age as his wife (twenty-six) and is a strong, healthy-looking, working-class man, very dark, with black hair and a swarthy complexion. He was a bit shy at first, but soon opened out during the interview. They were both pleased to accept the offer and we quickly settled details about times and the starting date (three days from this interview). Without being asked directly, Mr. V. told me of his opinions about Andy's difficulties and how they affected his wife and him. He saw the main difficulty in the whole situation as being the fact that they live in his parents' home. This leads to unhappiness and uncertainty in his wife's mind about her handling of Andy. He emphasized that his homelife has always been an unhappy one as far back as he can remember. He thought his parents should have separated long ago, but his mother always said that if they separated, *her* mother would die of the shock. He thought this was a ridiculous reason for staying together. His father is a mean man. Here Mrs. V. interjected: "He is more than mean, he is peculiar" and went on to give an example of this: when she broke her arm she had to go into the hospital and was making arrangements for the care of Andy, who was only a few months old at the time. Her father-in-law insisted that Andy be given to *his* mother, an old woman of nearly eighty, to be looked after. When Mrs. V. refused to do this, he burst into tears, had a temper tantrum, and threatened to commit suicide—"if that's not peculiar, I don't know what is." Mr. V. agreed and said that his father should have seen a psychiatrist years ago. But he obviously saw that there had to be an explanation of their remaining in such a disturbed household for the whole of their married life so far, and he went on to give it. Throughout the whole of this explanation I had the feeling that neither of them was convinced that it is the true explanation, i.e., that they were at least vaguely aware that it is a rationalization of a situation which they do not understand. This explanation was based on their lack of money and his inability to save toward getting their own home; the difficulties of paying the high rents demanded nowadays from a weekly wage of £12 to 13 (and this only if he works extra shifts); how the only occasion when they had a chance of getting a small flat at a reasonable rent came to nothing, because it came at a moment when they were awaiting the result of his application for a job outside London. They turned down the chance of the flat and in the event he did not get the job either. He does the rounds of the house agents nearly every week, but with no success. There is a basis of reality in these difficulties, of course, but it seems that his tie to the parents is not broken and that part of the work in this case will have to be on this.

He also referred to his wife's unfortunate early experiences, that they had left their mark on her, and that is why he would like help for Andy, so that he could escape such consequences —"these things are never forgotten and I think if you can do something about them at the time, it's far better."

He spoke of Andy's difficulties in getting to sleep, confirming his wife's account of this, but adding that he thought his wife was a bit too quick in taking Andy into their bed when he would not go to sleep again after waking during the night. When Andy comes into their bed there is no sleep for any of them after that, because he likes to thresh about the bed and cannot do this without keeping all three awake. He could see how difficult it is for her to leave Andy in his own bed, because he cries so much if he is left there, and of course Mr. V. does not get as much of this disturbance as his wife does, because he does night shifts frequently.

I said that I would like all four of us to have a part in the treatment. Mrs. V. would, of course, be bringing Andy to treatment and would be present, at least during the beginning phase of it. Perhaps Mr. V. too could come along to the Clinic occasionally when he is on night shifts, as this week, and we could discuss how things are going. He was pleased at this and assured me he would like to come along any time I wanted him to do so.

CHAPTER 5

THE WEEKLY REPORTS ON ANDY'S TREATMENT

WEEKLY REPORT NO. 1

SESSIONS 1 TO 5   *Age 2 years and 5 months*

During this first week of the analysis, Andy's mother has been present at all sessions, and I have made no attempt to separate them. On one occasion, however, during the first session when Andy and I left the treatment room to fetch some toy animals, Mrs. V. told him she would wait in the room until we returned. Andy insisted on her coming with us, and she did this with no more ado.

At sessions Mrs. V. is mostly silent and does not interfere verbally with Andy's activities, although it is obvious that she is uneasy about some of them. She makes comments following some of my interpretations, particularly if she can confirm their correctness from her own observations, and she also speaks of her own feelings in relation to Andy.

Andy had been attracted to the toys at the preliminary interview and at the first session he headed for the room in which the interview had been held. When I said that we would be going to another room, he said, "We are not going to the toys?" It was obvious that he felt very positively toward me during this first week, and he made many attempts to get close to me physically and to involve me as a playmate

in various games, e.g., he looked appealingly at me and repeated time and again in a very wheedling voice, "You play
with me"; at the end of the first session he wanted to know
whether I was coming when they left the treatment room;
later in the week, he took my hand on coming downstairs;
at another session he played a game which involved putting
all the toys inside my jacket as I sat on the couch beside
him, and during this game he leaned against me. The seductiveness of the situation was in danger of becoming mutual
when, in my ignorance, I made a response to his hurting himself by saying, "Poor Andy's hand, kiss-kiss better" and he
naturally presented his hand to be made better. I had made
this response as if he had been my own child, but fortunately
saw the error and it was not repeated. This mistake could
have had repercussions not only in the relationship with
Andy, but also with Mrs. V., as I had taken her role of com-
forter from her at that moment.

Andy's principal game during the week involved putting
the toy animals on top of one another to give them a ride. He
made an immediate identification with one of the animals,
a horse, and the horse was gently treated, unlike the other
animals, e.g., it did not ride on the camel's back as the others
did, and consequently escaped falling off the table; again,
when he had put all the animals to bed, the horse was the
only one which was not thrown unceremoniously out of bed.
I interpreted this identification by saying that I thought the
gee-gee's name was Andy, and he replied, "Yeah, gee-gee's got
a bad cough." This incident led Mrs. V. to tell me something
of the attitude of Andy's grandparents to him. If he should
use a phrase which struck them as adult, they would get him
to repeat it endlessly for their amusement, and of course Andy
enjoyed this and it led to his "showing off." One such phrase
which he used was "My goodness."

Another game which was interpretable in terms of his
curiosity about, and wish to join, parental intercourse was
when he made a fence around the gee-gee and announced

that it was going to jump out. When he tried to do this, however, the horse got stuck and he became quite anxious, appeal-
ing to me to help him. Almost simultaneously with this appeal
he heard the sound of a typewriter in the distance and asked
what the noise was. I said that the gee-gee was like Andy, he
sometimes liked to get out of his place to be with the other
moo-cows (his name for animals). He replied that he liked to
get out, to jump out, but made no reply when I added that
sometimes Andy heard noises and wanted to know what they
were all about. During this session Andy said he wanted to
wee-wee, but when he returned with his mother she said that
he had not wee-weed because he was in such a hurry to get
back to the room. He picked up a piece of string and tried to
tie my hands. I said that Andy was tying me up to make sure
that I would not go away, so that I would always be there
when he came back, just as he sometimes worried that his
mummy might go away when he went to sleep. He responded
to this by tying his mother's hands. Mrs. V. agreed that he
probably *did* worry that she would not be there if he should
awake, so that when he cannot get to sleep and she thinks it
is because he is anxious in this particular way, she always
picks him up and holds him. She thought he must have missed
this when he was in the hospital, because babies cannot get
individual attention there.

On Thursday Andy started throwing things around the
room and when I said that he seemed to be angry, Mrs. V.
said that she was to blame for this, because she was so irritable
today that she smacked him. She was irritable because she
was really afraid of going home from the clinic in the dark
(the Thursday session is at 3:30 P.M.). She has always been
afraid of being outside in the dark, although it is all right
when there is another adult with her. I commented that she
herself had seen the connection between her fear and being
irritable, how closely fear and anger were sometimes connected, and that she probably had seen the same thing in
Andy. At this point, Andy brought the tiger to me and roared

at me. I said that the tiger seemed to be angry too and Andy said that the tiger "*is* angry, so he has got to go to bye-byes." I said that with Andy it was the other way about and he replied, "Mummy said Andy's got to go to bye-byes and I don't want to." I said that sometimes Andy did not want to go to bye-byes because he was afraid his mummy might not be there if he woke up, so he got angry because he was frightened. Mrs. V. "confessed" that, in fact, on one occasion she and her husband had left him asleep in the care of his granny and he had awakened and been very frightened.

Summary

A good start on the whole, despite my technical errors. He shows an ability and readiness to act out in play his wishes and conflicts and to respond verbally to interpretations, directing these back from the toys to himself. There are many intercourse fantasies, with himself mostly in the role of the observer.

WEEKLY REPORT NO. 2
SESSIONS 6 TO 10

There has been much movement (metaphorically and literally) in the treatment this week. In the first three sessions Andy started off each day by throwing toys around the room and banging things on the table, making such a noise that his mother and I could not hear each other. I interpreted this as his wish to make so much noise that his mummy and I should not be able to talk; he did not want me to talk to her because he wanted her all to himself, he loved her so much. This was followed by a diminution of his demands on me during that session. Mrs. V. said she thought he was not in a good mood today because he was sleepy. At each session she reported that he had been sleeping all through each night this week, but had not been going to bed until very late (between 9 and 10:30 P.M.). This late bed-going had been in response to a suggestion I made that for the time being it would be a good idea not to focus the difficulty about bed on his having a fixed bedtime, but to let him find his own level, i.e., to put him to bed when he seemed sleepy, and that this might help us by clarifying the real "battle ground."

The following day she reported that Andy had bitten his three-year-old cousin the day before, that the boy had not retaliated (he never does apparently), and that she herself had had a row with the boy's mother, her sister, because immediately after Mrs. V. had told her sister how she hated Andy using "that word" (fuck) her sister had also used it. Mrs. V. recognized this as *unconscious* aggression on her sister's part, and it produced material relating to her compulsive daily visit to this sister, for fear the sister may come to harm if she does not visit. I interpreted this compulsion as a form of magic protection of her sister against Mrs. V.'s unconscious aggression. She smiled and said that it is quite true that she does not visit because she is fond of her sister; indeed, in many ways she dislikes her very much. Her sister is expecting another baby and I said that perhaps Andy's biting expresses his dislike of the idea of another baby coming. As soon as I said this to her, Andy picked up the "baby moo-cow" and threw it to the other end of the room, shouting, "Fuck the Pope." I told him that he worried in case his mother has another baby instead of him. He fell against the couch at this and started to whimper, going to his mother to be comforted. I said that Andy was showing us he is still mummy's baby, but really mummy would still love him even if one day she did have another baby. Mrs. V. grimaced at this and whispered that she would not have another one if she thought it would be like Andy. I said that she might change her mind when she started to feel easier about Andy.

On Wednesday there was more banging and throwing by him, and his mother winced at each blow. Repeated interpretation of his wish to keep us apart made no difference on that occasion. Mrs. V. suddenly "remembered" that there is another room in her in-laws' house which is not used and which could possibly be used as a separate bedroom for Andy. She wondered whether there would be trouble with him if he moved into another room. I said that I was sure there would be trouble, but it would be worth it, and that the move should be made while he is still in treatment so that we could deal with it together.

On Thursday both parents were present during the session, as we had arranged before treatment started. At this session we arranged that when Mr. V. starts night shift after Christmas he will come alone so that I could get his slant on things. Mr. V. was very restrictive with Andy during the session, interfering with his aggressive play, but when Andy said "Fuck it," Mr. V. laughed and looked at me to see my reaction. Mrs. V. reported that Andy does not now use "that word" anywhere except in his session, and that he is naughty only in sessions now. I explained why I did not discourage his activities during sessions, at the same time saying that I recognized how relieved she must be that the naughtiness is contained in a situation where it can be understood and interpreted to him. Mr. V. explained that they had to stop his throwing things at home, because there is so much glass in their tiny rooms. I said that this was perfectly understandable, but as Andy is a developing child and has a need for activity, there is a very strong argument in favor of their moving to a house of their own where he would have more freedom. Mrs. V. proudly announced that they had made the arrangements about Andy having a bedroom of his own. Mr. V. spoke of his wife mentioning to him that I thought Andy tried to monopolize me so that I could not talk to his mother, and that he (Mr. V.) had noticed how Andy did the same thing whenever he and his wife were talking. I remarked that Andy also interrupted them during the night by waking up and Mr. V. said that perhaps Andy thinks they are hurting each other. During this time Andy had been playing quietly with the animals, but when his father made the remark about hurting each other, he picked up a "lady doll" and tried to undress it "to give her a wash." I said to Mr. V. that Andy likes to know everything that's going on and that he would like to see his mummy without her clothes and give *her* a wash. His mother immediately remarked, before Andy could open his mouth, that he had never seen her in her bath but that he sometimes went into the bathroom when his daddy was there. Mr. V. said that he didn't see the point of hiding things from Andy, but that maybe this is a wrong point of view. I said that I thought it a good idea to be honest with Andy, but there is always the danger of stimulating his curiosity too much and exciting him more than he can cope with without anxiety. Andy was by now playing with a toy telephone, saying, "Hello, fuckie piggie, hello fuckie bogie" and looking at me very provocatively. I said to him that he was saying "Fuckie" because his mummy and daddy said it is naughty and he wonders what *I* will say. At this, Mrs. V. wondered whether he would become more naughty during some part of the treatment. I said I thought that he was testing me out, to see in which things I agreed with his mummy and daddy and those in which I disagreed; after all, there are differences between treatment and home, and we must help him sort out the differences.

The Friday session saw a big step for Mrs. V. and Andy. At her own suggestion Mrs. V. left the treatment room, saying that she would wait downstairs until Andy and I were finished. Andy said this was "all right," but ten minutes later he wanted to wee-wee; however, his mother reported afterwards that he had not in fact urinated. I said to both of them that Andy was just making sure that she was still there. When Andy and I were alone again he played with the lady doll, but this time he was much more direct in his curiosity, saying that he wanted to see the lady's knickers.

Summary

The parents are making good use of the treatment by discussing and observing. They are also taking practical steps to alter the sleeping arrangements. Andy's aggression is coming within therapeutic range instead of being acted out at home to the same degree. His sexual curiosity is being acted out in play with the doll.

WEEKLY REPORT NO. 3

Sessions 11 to 15

Most of the sessions are now spent without Mrs. V. being in the room. Sometimes Andy asks her to come upstairs to the treatment room with us, but after a few minutes he acquiesces when she leaves, after telling him she will wait downstairs for him. Sometimes he leaves the waiting room without her.

On Monday he was tearing at the lady doll's clothes and biting it, saying that he was "biting her belly off." I said that he thought the lady had a baby inside her, just like Auntie, and he responded by saying furiously, "Fuck it," and throwing the doll away. The doll hit a tumbler and produced a ringing noise; Andy said, "Oh, my goodness, you frightened me out of your life." I said that he was so angry that he frightened himself, but he didn't frighten me and I would certainly not leave him because he was angry. He came very close to me and shouted "Fuckie, fuckie" into my face, and I added that he was trying to see if he could really upset me because he worried that his mummy might leave him when he upset her. He danced around the room shouting "Fuckie, fuckie," but it was more like a song than an oath.

The following day he told his mother to stay in the waiting room as he was "going to play with his doctor friend." In the treatment room he again threw things around. I did not intervene in any way and finally he got hold of the gee-gee and the baby moo-cow, saying they were going for a walk down a red road to a red park. He handed me the baby moo-cow and he showed me what I was to do with it. We were to cradle the animals in our arms and rock them, saying, "Go to sleep, little one." I said that the little ones went to sleep, each in his own little room. He put the gee-gee down on the table and brought the mother moo-cow over and placed it beside the gee-gee, but with a piece of fencing between them, saying, "And the mummy sleeps there." I said that she slept nearby so that she could hear the little one if he should get frightened. At the end of the session he said, "Good-night, Mr. Bogie-boogie" instead of his usual "Bye-bye."

On Wednesday Mrs. V. was present for about the first fifteen minutes of the session before she moved out. Andy played with the gee-gee and a tumblerful of water, putting the gee-gee into the water and then taking it out and sucking it. His mother obviously disapproved, but said nothing about it. She was pleased to report that last night Andy actually asked her to leave him so that he could go to sleep. She shame-facedly said that she had shaken him yesterday for using "that word." She cannot ignore it and in fact, for the first time in her life, she gave her sister a good telling off for using such language in front of Andy. Her sister was angry, and normally this would have frightened Mrs. V., but she persisted, telling her sister that if she did not stop using this language when Andy is present she would not visit any more. I commented that she now seemed able to allow herself to feel aggressive, without being so guilty about it, and she said that she had surprised herself, but felt a lot better when she had really spoken her mind for once. I laughed and added, "And she didn't fall down dead." She again reported some improve-ment in Andy's behavior at home.

On Thursday Andy told me a story: "Once upon a time a little boy went for a walk down a road and he met a gee-gee and the gee-gee bit him and the little boy said fuck and told the gee-gee to get out." When I commented that he did not like the idea of being bitten, he bit the toy gee-gee and threw it away. I said that he thought he might get bitten by the gee-gee because he wanted to bite the gee-gee. He began once more to throw things about and at the end of the session ran straight into the wall, bumping his head. He started to cry and I took him to his mother, saying that his mummy would soon make him better, but that I thought he had hurt himself because he was afraid of hurting somebody else.

On Friday there were many aggressive games and he continually invited me to join in these. There were indications that he often plays such games with somebody at home, probably his grandfather or father.

Summary

An improvement is reported in the sleeping situation and also in the aggressive behavior at home. The aggression is related to oedipal fantasies, with the possibility that he uses the defense of turning aggression against the self.

WEEKLY REPORT NO. 4

Sessions 16 to 20

Mrs. V. reported that Andy now has a bedroom of his own. On the first few nights of sleeping in his own room he had awakened during the night, but no oftener than usual; on the fifth night he had slept the whole night through—the first time he had done this since he was a few days old. She was very pleased with this and thought it marvelous. However, his grandparents were said to be furious at the idea of his being put in a room of his own, saying that all children went through this phase of disturbed sleep and he would grow out of it. She was able to tell them that Andy is *her* child and she wishes him to sleep in his own room. I inquired about the kind of games Andy plays with the grownups at home and she told me he plays all sorts of exciting, rough games with his grandfather, and is encouraged to hurt his grandfather as much as he likes.

His favorite activity at the beginning of the week was the usual one of throwing toys around the room, aiming some of them at me. I told him often that I would not allow him to hurt me or himself and at first he told me to shut up, but he changed to playing traveling games with his cars.

He played out many anal intercourse fantasies with the cars, animals, and dolls, and these were interpreted as his doing to them what he thought his daddy did to his mummy in bed. His immediate response to this was to scatter the animals and to say that they were dead. I said that Andy liked to think he could tell the animals to do what he wanted, just as he would like his daddy and mummy to do what he wanted. The following day he reclined on the couch and asked me to tell him a story. I told him about a little boy who was very rough and noisy and sometimes got frightened at his rough-ness and noisiness, but his friend told him he would not let him hurt himself or his friend. When I asked for a story in return, he repeated the story of the little boy and the gee-gee, then stood up and held his penis, saying that he would put a pin in his winkie; then he changed his mind and said that he would put a pin in my winkie. I told him nobody would hurt his winkie, neither his daddy nor anybody else. At the end of that session he stood at the top of the stairs and pretended to be about to fall, but he made sure that I was near enough to catch him.

The following day I had to restrain him physically as he started pulling violently on the not-too-secure wash basin. This was the morning on which his mother had reported the first full night's sleep; so when he asked for a story, I told him of the little boy who used to be frightened during the night, but when he knew that his mummy was very near his bedroom if he wanted her, he was not frightened any more and slept through the whole night. His story in reply was short and simple: "Somebody put a pin in a little boy's winkie." When he told me this story, he rushed to the door, saying he wanted a wee-wee. I went downstairs immediately after him, saying we would ask his mummy to help him, but he went straight to the toilet and managed to do it himself, but he commanded me to pull the plug. I said that he had got frightened at the idea of anybody putting a pin in his winkie and hurting it, so he had wanted a wee-wee just to see if his winkie was still working. I discovered from his mother that he had seen a cousin having his nappies changed the other day and that he had been fascinated.

Summary

Mrs. V. is beginning to assert herself with her in-laws, but they obviously play a very disturbing part in Andy's development, especially the grandfather.

Andy shows his aggressive anal intercourse fantasies. His castration fears and wishes are intermingled, the fears being seen as a turning against the self of his wishes, i.e., castration as a talion punishment.

WEEKLY REPORT NO. 5

SESSIONS 21 TO 25   *Age 2 years and 6 months*

The intercourse fantasies were again played out in sessions, but now the idea that babies are made by intercourse was more clearly seen, together with his wish that he remain his mother's only baby.

At the first session of the week, while he was playing with the animals, he described the baby moo-cow as a "sister baby." When I asked whether he knew anybody who had one, he said that George, his cousin, had one and that George is greedy. (I learned from Mrs. V. at the end of this session that George's mother has been admitted to the hospital for the birth of her baby and that due to a misunderstanding Mrs. V. had been told that a girl had been born. Andy had been told this, but when they discovered that the baby was not yet born they did not tell him, to avoid confusing him—they are hoping that the baby *will* be a girl!) Andy then crashed the cars and animals together and I told him that he was playing at making a baby, adding that he thought that was how his mummy and daddy made babies, by crashing together. He shouted "Fuck" at me and threw the animals around. When I said that Andy did not want a sister baby, he shouted "Yes, yes, yes" but acted "No, no, no."

Before and after every session for the rest of the week Andy went up and down the stairs on his knees, a not inconsiderable balancing feat when going down. I interpreted this as his showing what a little baby he is and that he wants to be the only baby in his house, that he does not want another baby there. He was very peremptory with his mother, ordering her to come upstairs with us to the treatment room, and as soon as we arrived ordering her back downstairs. I said that he was trying to show us who is boss, to tell himself that his mummy does exactly as he wishes, so that he can be sure that if he does not want her to have a baby, she will do as she is told. After that he did not insist on her coming up.

During one session he wanted me to play a crashing game with him and when I said he would like us to make a baby together, he put the cars and animals into the wastepaper basket, saying he was putting them into the potty. I said that he thought he could make babies like jobbies, whereupon he rattled them about in the basket, made the magic incantation "Fuckie bogie" over them, then sat on the basket and grinned at me.

I asked Mrs. V. to stay during the next session, and after Andy had said that the lady doll had a pin in her bum and I interpreted this as a game of making babies, she protested that he could not possibly know about such things, as he had never once awakened when she and her husband had intercourse. I said that it would be impossible for her to be sure of this, but in any case he would be bound to have fantasies concerning what they did in bed together. Andy then took a hand in this by telling us to stop talking and then made sure of interrupting us by pulling off the towel rail and then attacking the wash basin. Then he stood up on the couch and said he would fall off, but instead he came down, put a cushion on the floor and fell on that! I told Mrs. V. that I

thought the grandfather's games with Andy were too stimulating and that I thought she should find some way of stopping them. She said that she thinks the grandfather is mad.
(Whenever Mr. and Mrs. V. talk of leaving, the grandfather
talks of committing suicide. Before Andy's birth the grandfather had even made some suicidal gestures which Mrs. V.
dismissed as such, saying that if he really had wanted to kill
himself, there was ample opportunity to do so. Since Andy
was born he declares that Andy is his whole life, and if they
go he will have nothing left to live for.) I said that he seemed
to be using Andy for his own purposes, in ways which are
definitely prejudicial to Andy's healthy development. She
said that recently, when he was trying to interfere between
Andy and her, she told him to mind his own business; there
was a terrible scene: the grandfather cried and stormed at
her, saying that she was trying to finish him off. I commented
that there could be no stronger argument for them to move
out of that house at the earliest possible moment. She told
me they have been going the rounds of the housing agents
regularly once more, but so far without success. She also reported that although Andy's sleep is once more disturbed, he
does not now need to see her—when he awakes she calls out
to him that she is there, and he goes back to sleep immediately. I complimented her on her handling of this, saying that
she is doing very well. During this long talk Andy had been
quietly playing a farm game with the animals, spreading them
over the couch to graze on the grass.

Summary

Andy tries to deal with his anxiety about being displaced
by another baby by behaving like a baby and also by trying
to prove and exercise his omnipotence. He is not averse, however, to trying to produce babies himself, and these are anal
babies.

Details were produced of the disturbing and disturbed be-

havior of the grandfather, with whom Andy has a sadomasochistic relationship.

WEEKLY REPORT NO. 6

Sessions 26 to 29

Andy has spent almost as much time on the stairs this week
as he has in the treatment room. He literally crawls upstairs,
asking me occasionally to pick him up and carry him. Coming
down he has various methods, not including walking, e.g.,
on his knees, on his back, on his front. Often when he comes
to a landing, he turns back and repeats the process on the
same flight of stairs. He had also tried to pull off the stars
attached to the staircase above the Christmas tree. His behavior before and after sessions has been very provocative
and his mother reports that he has been equally provocative
to her at home, inviting punishment which she is sometimes
unable to refrain from dealing out. At first I saw this behavior as a continuation of the theme of the previous week,
in which he was insisting that he should be the only baby,
but eventually other factors emerged and these were that he
invites punishment as a means of controlling his aggressive
impulses and also that smacking is part of his intercourse
fantasies, so that if he is smacked he is making a baby with
the smacker. These became clearer in his play with the animals during the session when he scolded a moo-cow for being
a naughty fuckie, then smacked it and put it to bye-byes,
saying that now he could not be naughty. Again while playing with a moo-cow he smacked it and then put a baby moo-
cow beside it, saying, "There's a sister baby now" and then
put the baby in the wastepaper basket. He then turned to me
with a wheedling smile and said, "*You* do it to *me* now," and
when I asked what he wanted me to do, he said, "Tell me
fuckie, fuckie, don't be naughty."

On the last day of the term Mrs. V. told me that she had
been feeling so nervous that she had gone to see her family

doctor. I then learned for the first time that she had been having sedatives prescribed for some time, but that now the doctor had said that she should go to see a psychiatrist. Mrs. V. had said, however, that she is seeing me to get help for Andy and that she would speak to me about it first. I suggested that we should try to get our earlier arrangement into operation as soon as possible, i.e., that when her husband is on night shift they will both come to the Clinic with Andy and that I would see her alone after Andy's session, and also her husband occasionally. This has not been possible so far, as Mr. V. has been working much overtime during the Christmas rush, but it should be possible to start early next term. She was much reassured by this, although I think it is probably a manifestation of her jealousy of Andy, as well as a genuine wish for help.

Summary

Andy's provocative behavior is seen as a wish for his aggressive impulses to be controlled through punishment by an external agency, as well as part of his intercourse fantasies.

Mrs. V. appeals directly for help for herself, partly in opposition to Andy's need.

There will be a break of ten days for the Christmas holiday.

WEEKLY REPORT NO. 7

SESSIONS 30 TO 34   *Age 2 years and 7 months*

The sessions restarted more or less where we had left off before the holiday. On the first day Andy stood at the bottom of the stairs and asked to be picked up, as he is a little baby. I told him that he is not really a little baby, but he would like to be mummy's *only* little boy. He promptly walked upstairs and has stopped crawling up and down stairs since then, except on one occasion when he came down one flight on his bottom. The crashing games were in evidence a great deal that first day, but the simple crashing became elaborated into a game in which the gee-gee's front legs were attached to the back of an aeroplane and this was pulled along the table. He said that there was a little baby in the plane, and I interpreted the game as one in which he plays at making babies—the gee-gee is the daddy, the plane is the mummy, and the baby is made inside the mummy. He insisted that I should do the same with a tiger and another plane, and I said that he would like to make a baby with me. He repeated that there is a little baby inside the plane, and I said that he was wondering whether his mummy has a little baby inside her. He said she hadn't and started to throw the toys around. At the end of this session Mrs. V. told me that they had had a good holiday and that Andy had slept well and had been well-behaved (more or less).

At the next sessions he again played violently, then he changed to a game in which he dropped the gee-gee repeatedly into a tumblerful of water, saying, "Plop, plop" all the time. Once he wanted me to play the same game, and I said that he wanted me to play the same kind of games with him that his grandpa does.

On Thursday he yelled himself red in the face. For practically the whole session he shouted "Shut up" at me, and I understood this in terms of his wish for his mother and me to have no communication whatsoever. He had insisted on her coming upstairs and would not let her leave the room; but whenever she or I spoke, he yelled at *me*. He stood in the middle of the room with his arms folded, puffing through his nose, getting redder and redder in the face. Then he started incanting his list of swear words, "Fuck, fuckie, fuckin' 'ell, blimey, kick you in the ear 'ole," repeating this over and over again. I said to him that he was angry because his mother and I were talking, as he wanted to be the only one to say anything. Suddenly he introduced a new factor. He lay back on the couch and said that his daddy had gone to work to get his money, and a few seconds later that his daddy is going away on a boat and he doesn't like his daddy.

I asked him who says that; after telling me to shut up, he said his grandpa says it. (I took this to mean that his grandpa had told him that his daddy wants to go away on a boat [to Canada] and I thought the implication was that *grandpa* would be left behind.) I thought this fitted in with what Mr. and Mrs. V. had already told me about the grandfather, so I spoke again to Mrs. V. about the importance of their getting away from the grandfather and his interference in their relationships.

On Friday Mrs. V. warned me in the waiting room that Andy was likely to prove difficult that day as he had not wanted to come to the Clinic. On the contrary, he was most docile. When I collected his toy box from the cupboard, he slipped under my arm and grabbed a doll and took it upstairs with him. He spent the whole session dressing and undressing the doll, washing it, putting it to bed and so on. First of all he laid it on its face, pulled down its knickers, and said, "That's her bum." He referred to the doll as "he" or "she," apparently indiscriminately. I asked what name he would give to the doll and he said "Andy V.—no—Whisky V.," then, "Is a sister baby and wants to wee-wee!" He pointed to the doll's nonexistent winkie, saying, "That's her winkie," insisting that she had one even when I said that little girls don't have winkies like little boys. When I remarked that he did not like the idea of girls and mummies not having winkies like boys and daddies, he smacked the doll, telling her that she had been naughty. Then he turned to me and smiled, saying, "I didn't want to kick you yesterday, I'm sorry." I said that he sometimes wanted to kick me when he was annoyed with me, and I knew how hard it was for him not to kick me sometimes; in any case I would make sure he did not hurt me. When he is angry with me, it is all right for him to tell me so. He took the doll home with him that day and we carried it downstairs between us, as he insisted we must help the little baby downstairs because she is too little to walk down alone.

Summary

An elaboration of the anal intercourse fantasies, but with a reduction of the aggressive content of these fantasies. He also expresses anxiety about his father's hypothetical departure, and this is associated in his fantasy with father's sexual relationship with mother. He shows denial of the absence of a penis in the female. I think the play with the doll shows, among other things, the beginnings of reaction formation against his aggression toward his rivals (father and a possible sibling).

WEEKLY REPORT NO. 8

SESSIONS 35 TO 39

The focal point of his behavior during sessions this week has been the doll, which he washes, dresses, and undresses. He named the doll "Andrew V." (not "Andy" for some reason) and at the beginning of the week treated it quite gently. On Tuesday, when his father came to the Clinic with him and Mrs. V., Andy insisted on his coming to the session with us, and would not let him leave the room for about the first half hour. Although Andy's behavior during the session was much more restrained than when he is alone with me, Mr. V. was much more restrictive than his wife, who depends on me to set the limits of what Andy can or cannot do. Mr. V. gave the opinion that when there is an upset in the family, it is much more due to his wife than to Andy. He thinks she makes too much fuss of Andy, that he is more strict, and that Andy reacts better to firmness than to being allowed to do whatever he likes. I said to Mr. V. that perhaps he thought that I allowed Andy to do things of which Mr. V. did not approve, but I explained to him, as I had previously explained to his wife, the reasons for my not discouraging certain activities during sessions. I also took the opportunity of giving him my opinion of the effect on Andy of living with his grandparents.

He told me that just that day they had heard of a possible flat—his wife had heard last night of a woman dying and had gone round first thing this morning to the agents for the letting of the dying woman's house!

Andy spent the whole of the Wednesday session washing, first the doll and then the gee-gee. He kept turning to me with a pleased smile, but I had no indication of the fantasy in the play except that in the past the gee-gee has represented himself. I supposed that he was playing at being mummy to my daddy, but did not interpret. At the end of this session, as I was stooping down to pick up a toy from the floor, he put his arms round my neck and said, "I love you." This declaration was followed the next morning by an incident again showing his wish for intimacy. Just as I opened the door of the waiting room, Andy and his mother were coming out. Mrs. V. said that Andy had just told her he wanted to wee-wee. Andy immediately took his hand away from her and took mine instead, saying, "My friend will do it for me." He was visibly peeved when I said that his mummy would help him, although I thought he could now do it without help. Mrs. V. confirmed that he usually does so at home, although he will occasionally ask for help. During the session he washed a doll, but then abandoned it in favor of the lady doll. He washed this, then pulled up the skirt, saying, "Let's look at her bum, stick a pin in her bum, take her clothes off." I related this to the invitation to help him in the lavatory by saying that he wanted to look at my bum and to stick a pin in my bum, and that I should look at his bum and stick a pin in it—in other words, he wanted us to do together what he thinks his parents do. He neither confirmed nor denied this, but became very excited and started splashing the water out of the wash basin. I told him that he should keep the water inside; when he persisted in splashing, I warned him that I would have to let the water run away if he did not keep it in the basin, and later I did let the water run away. He cried bitterly at this and came over to me and put his head on my knee, but soon recovered after I had said that I would like him to be able to play, but I could not allow him to splash the water on the floor like that, and that he could pretend that there was water in the bath. He continued to play at "washing" the lady doll and then became once more interested in taking her clothes off. At the end of the session he wanted to wee-wee again, but after I had said he wanted me to help him so that I could see what a nice winkie he has, he walked past the toilet. When I said to his mother that he wanted to wee-wee again, he said that he did not want to now.

The Friday session was another washing day, although he said at the beginning that I should shut my mouth. He again splashed water on the floor, but desisted when I said that he remembered that I had said I could not allow him to do this yesterday and he was wondering whether I would stop him today.

Summary

Andy's role seems to have shifted somewhat from being the baby to his becoming the mother. At first he (the mother) looks after himself (the baby), but then he wants to make a baby with me which we can both look after. He tries to make love to me by wanting me to see his winkie and to see him urinate; the water play is apparently associated with urethral fantasies.

At the practical level, the parents seem to be becoming more active in their search for a home of their own.

WEEKLY REPORT NO. 9

SESSIONS 40 TO 44   *Age 2 years and 8 months*

He was very concerned about messing and cleanliness at the beginning of the week, in this way identifying with the mother. He spent the first two sessions at the sink, washing cars, puppets, animals, and so on, but not the doll. When I stopped his splashing the water around on the floor, he was very annoyed with me and said so. Another game he played at was clearing out his locker with sweeps of his hand, scattering everything on the floor, washing and then returning everything to the cupboard. I remarked that he wanted to show me that he could make things clean as well as dirty. During these washing sessions he kept turning to me with a very pleased smile on his face, obviously looking for my approval. On the stairs, before and after sessions, he took the opportunity to tell all the passers-by that they stink, and he wanted me to say that they stink.

On Wednesday he would not come upstairs alone with me and also refused to come up with his mother; he wanted to stay downstairs with the receptionist. However, when I said that he wanted to show his mummy and me that he could tell us to do what he wanted, but that it was not true that we could do only what *he* told us to do, and that his mother and I were going upstairs whether he wanted to come or not, he followed behind us. Every time I looked around to see whether he was coming, he shouted "Shut up" at me. On one of these occasions a member of the office staff was passing us as he shouted "Shut up" and she asked him whether he meant her to shut up. He replied, indignantly, "No, my *friend* is to shut up." Mrs. V. left the room in a few minutes when Andy was occupied washing. Contrary to his usual protests when the sink plug is put in, he was quite amenable. He bit the washing cloth, drank soapy water, and tried to put his head into the water. When he started splashing the water onto the floor, I reminded him that the water was to be kept inside the basin and he said "Sorry," but he could not control his wish to let the water out. He told me to shut up, but he quite amiably helped me to dry the floor and put away the toys at the end of the session.

Thursday was another washing session, but this time he told me to sit on the couch and read the comic papers he had brought with him, while he did the washing. He kept on

saying "Fuck" and drew my attention to this each time, saying, "I said fuck again." He was enjoying this so much that
I said that he was saying fuck because he wanted me to like
it. He invited me to say it also. Then he went to the cupboard and threw everything out and dashed backward and
forward, dropping toys into the water, saying "Plunk,
plunk." He was very excited, and I said that he was playing
at doing poo-poos in the potty, and when he invited me to
say "Plunk, plunk," I added that he wanted me to like his
poo-poos. He ran toward me and went through the motions
of putting on my "knackies," saying, "Poo, you stink." I
said that he likes me, so thinks that I stink, because he likes
stinking things. At this he said that he wanted to wee-wee,
and we went downstairs to get his mother to take him to the
toilet. However, when we were half way down he started to
whimper, as he had urinated in his trousers. I said it was
alright as I knew he wee-weed like a big boy most of the time,
but sometimes he forgot and did it in his trousers.

On Friday the central play was with the doll again, which
was very much "our baby," and he not only washed and dried
her, dressed and undressed her, but sat her on the wastepaper
basket to do wee-wees and poo-poos. When I interpreted this
as his pretending that the dolly is our baby because he would
like so much to be able to make a baby with me, he talked of
monkeys throwing rocks at him, trying to hit him on the
belly, to hit him on the winkie. I interpreted this as his fear
of his winkie getting hurt if anybody knew of his wish to
make a baby with his mummy; following this, he fell to the
floor and declared that he was dead.[1]

WEEKLY REPORT NO. 10

SESSIONS 45 TO 49

This week he has elaborated on the castration fantasies which
were hinted at last week in association with the wish to make

[1] From this date on Summaries were not made.

babies. A favorite gesture on the way upstairs to treatment is to put his hand through the banisters to "shoot" various monkeys and wolves that are lurking about. He also "shoots" any men we may meet on the stairs, but not the women, to whom he is abusive rather than lethal. At several sessions he extended these fantasies in his play, in which he has again started using the toy animals. He frequently mentioned a big wolf up a tree which would jump down and bite the little wolf "on the ear'ole or on the belly or on his winkie." At first, when I tried to elucidate the reasons for the big wolf's attacks, Andy said that he did all these things because "he wanted to," but gradually the stories changed to the point that the big wolf *wanted* to do all these things to the little wolf, but could not because the little wolf would not let him. I interpreted at this point only that the little wolf is Andy, who is afraid somebody might hurt him, and he confirmed this by saying, "I wouldn't let him"; but finally we saw quite clearly one of the origins of his castration fear, viz., his wish to castrate the father. When I asked why the big wolf was up the tree, Andy triumphantly replied, "Because I chased him up." There were many games of fighting between the toy tigers, the little one invariably defeating the big one. In conjunction with the castration material in the play and fantasies, he also acted out the same theme in some measure in the transference. On the way upstairs he showed considerable reluctance to come to the room, and dawdled as much as he could. During sessions he tended to be what was, for him, conciliatory. After sessions he was usually very provocative, trying to take as long as possible to go downstairs, playing with light switches, etc. I think these different attitudes indicated his fear of me in the transference, and also his way of trying to cope with his fear by displaying his power over me when it seemed safe to do so, viz., *after* the session.

WEEKLY REPORT NO. 11

Sessions 50 to 54

As in previous sessions, the outstanding castration fantasies are almost always played out on the stairs, either on the way to or from the session. This takes the form of unwillingness to come to sessions, lying "dead" on the landings, shooting monkeys, tigers and wolves through the banister, shooting the men he meets. His choice of toy to bring to sessions has changed back to motor cars and motor bikes and he has abandoned the doll altogether.

In contrast to this behavior on the stairs, he was "very good" in the treatment room at the beginning of the week. He played endless games of going to bed on the couch, crashing games with the motor cars, clearing out the locker and then replacing everything. I call this "very good" as the acting out of his fantasies in this way did not involve, for him, a direct attack on me, nor was it provocative, as so much of his stair behavior is.

On Thursday and Friday, however, a new feature appeared in his behavior. He stood in the center of the room screaming as loudly as he could. I thought this must have something to do with his mother being able to hear him (in fact, she confirmed that she had been able to hear him very well), but I was not sure what he wanted to convey to her, so merely said that he was screaming loudly so that his mummy would hear him. This met with reiterated screaming which he plainly enjoyed. I added that it made him feel good to know that his mummy could hear him, it was almost as if they were together. He stopped screaming, but I had no other indication of the correctness of my interpretation.

When I saw Mrs. V. on Tuesday, she spoke of Andy's recent concern about his winkie and she had remembered that this might be a "delayed reaction" to an experience he had had about six months before he started treatment, i.e., when he was twenty-two months old. She had noticed that he found urinating painful and when she took him to her doctor, she had been told that he required to be circumcised. However, when she took him to a surgical outpatient clinic, she was told that circumcision would not be necessary, but as there were adhesions these would be broken down at the clinic. Andy was removed to another room and she heard him screaming with pain. When she was allowed into the room with him, she saw that there had been two attendants holding him down while the doctor had been doing something to his penis. She was told to bring him back again, and in fact he attended this clinic twice more. He has had no difficulty in urinating since then, but she thought it must have been a terrifying experience for him.

WEEKLY REPORT NO. 12

SESSIONS 55 TO 59

In contrast to the rather stereotyped sessions of the last two weeks, these five sessions have been crammed with informative material. He came upstairs with no difficulty on Monday, although he paused momentarily to shoot some monkeys. He played mostly at opening and shutting his locker, then he spoke of the big tiger and the little tiger, how they hit one another. He had brought a Rupert book from the waiting room and looked at the pictures in this with great interest, his main interest being in a dragon, which he called a tiger. In one of the pictures he saw a baby and he drew my attention to this with an indulgent sound, "Aw, look at the little baby." I asked him whether he had seen George's sister baby yet, to which he replied, "Yes, but he's not George's sister baby, he's my sister baby." I said that the baby is a little girl, not "he," and I wondered whether he had seen the baby in her bath. He did not reply to this, but when I asked the mother at the end of the session whether Andy had seen the baby undressed, she said that he had not.

He brought a new toy motorbike to Tuesday's session and
played for some time with this "nice little bike," talking the
while of the tigers biting one another and of the wolves doing
the same. He went to bed on the couch. His flirtation was
continued, rather amusingly, in the form of his asking for a
cup of tea, then orange, then a blackcurrant drink. I commented on his playing at doing the same thing with me that
he does with his mummy at night before he goes to sleep in
his real bed. He said, "Yes, good-night, come on, come and
lie down beside me." I said that he wanted us to play at
doing the same thing that mummy and daddy do when they
go to bed, and this produced a very good-natured smile, accompanied by the endearment, "You fuckie bogie." He got
out of bed and resumed the play with the locker key, finally
putting all the keys up his jersey. I interpreted the likeness
of the key to his winkie and again he went to bed and invited
me to join him. He took off his shoes and once more I interpreted his wish to play at mummy and daddy. The frustration was too much for him and eventually led to much disappointment and hostility toward me, expressed at the end
of the session by kicking me at the side of the eye as I bent
down to tie his shoelace. I spontaneously said that I was very
annoyed with him and he nodded and said in a low voice,
"And *I'm* annoyed with you"—his whisper being much more
effective really than my loud voice. We went quietly and
quickly downstairs and he announced in a calm voice to his
mother that he had kicked me on the head.

I saw Mrs. V. alone that afternoon and she told me first of
all that she has finally agreed to think about the possibility
of their emigrating to Canada when Andy's treatment is
finished. She finds that Andy is turning more and more to
her, away from his grandparents, who get very annoyed with
him nowadays over very little. Andy frequently tells her he
loves her. I did not comment on the possible ambivalence
of this, but said how good it is that he is able to put his feel-

ings into words and how this augurs well for his future development.

I also said that I was glad to hear that Andy is turning more to her, and that she sounded pleased with this too. She agreed and went on to tell me that she had heard Andy screaming during his sessions last Thursday and Friday and that he had screamed in exactly the same way at home at the week end (I wondered whether this screaming is a way of obliterating separation—the week-end separation from me this time). Mrs. V., however, thought it was somehow connected with an incident last week. She was in another room and heard him start to cry. She went immediately into the room and found him with his grandfather. She asked the grandfather what had happened and he became abusive, telling her to shut up, it was none of her business. She told him that he was being absurd, her son *is* her business. He continued to shout at her and Andy went up to him and said, "Don't you shout at my mummy," and led his mother away from the grandfather. I said to Mrs. V. that this protective attitude toward her was another good sign of his ongoing development. His sleep is very good at the moment. He wakens during the night occasionally, but falls asleep again immediately when she lets him know she is nearby.

On Wednesday he would not come to the room with me until I said that he was still annoyed with me for being annoyed with *him* when he kicked my head. Then he came upstairs. As soon as we were inside he fell back against the couch and slid down to the floor, saying that the "little pussy is falling on his bottom, the little pussy has hurt his bottom, the little pussy is crying, poor little pussy—but the big wolf comes along and says 'Poor little pussy' and picks him up and carries him on his back and the little pussy is all right." He then went to the locker and got out two toy motor cars, dragged the small table round beside me and invited me to "play babbies," i.e., to crash our cars together.

The following dialogue then took place:

"You would really like us to make a babby together."

"Well, there's a little babby inside my car."

"You want to have a babby inside you, just like a mummy who has a babby inside her."

"*My* mummy don't have a babby inside her. She's got biscuits and apples and oranges inside her."

"Mummy has all the good things inside her—what does daddy have inside him?"

"Poo-poos! I want to wash now. No, I want to do poo-poos."

"You think you have a poo-poo babby inside you."

"No I don't, I've got *poo-poos* inside me."

The following day he would not come upstairs without his mother, but he allowed her to leave the treatment room within a few minutes, while he played at washing a toy lorry, biting the washing cloth and then hanging it out to dry. I remarked that he was playing at being the mummy. He stopped washing and lay down on the couch with his feet toward me. Then he drew his legs up, opened them and put his hands on his penis. I said that he was playing at doing what mummy does with daddy in bed and that he wanted me to do it with him. He said, "No, I'm not, give me your bleeding keys," and then got up and went to the locker, tried to open it for a few seconds, but gave up. He clutched at his penis again, saying, "Oh, me little winkie," to which I said that he wanted very much to play at being the mummy, but he is frightened that if he does this with me, he will lose his little winkie. He said, "The bleeding tiger will cut it off, but I won't let it." I assured him that he would not really have his winkie cut off even if he would like to make a baby, but at this point he slipped and banged his head against the wash basin and he started to cry bitterly. I said that poor Andy felt he would lose his winkie, so he hurts himself in the hope that the tiger will be satisfied with that and so that he can go down to his mummy and she will make his head better.

Friday saw his repeated assertion that making a baby is a

dirty and fierce proceeding. He washed away at the toy cars and after finishing with them he tidied up the floor. I remarked that he was doing all the things he had seen his mummy do at home. He then put a face cloth between his legs at the front and a floor cloth between his legs behind, declaring that these were poo-poos. I said that I thought he was playing at being the mummy who is making a baby and that making a baby is the same as making poo-poos. He yelled at me that I stink and started throwing everything out of the locker, shouting "Shut up" all the time. I remarked that he thought that making a baby is a noisy, dirty thing, but he wants to just the same.

WEEKLY REPORT NO. 13

SESSIONS 60 TO 64

Sessions this week have been dominated by play with motor cars, which he makes crash again and again. He has been unwilling to come to the sessions without his mother, although he usually acquiesces in her leaving the room after a few minutes. On one day this was not so, however, and he was really distressed when she left.

During the first three sessions of the week he played with the cars, either washing them or crashing them together. He invited me to crash the car he had allocated to me, and on one occasion forestalled my interpretation of the game, mentioning that there was a baby inside his car.

On Wednesday he handed me a Noddy glove-puppet from his locker and asked me to put it on. When I did so, however, he was a bit taken aback when it moved. He said to me, "Let him bite *your* finger." He would not have any contact with Noddy after having shaken hands with him. The indications were that Noddy might have been my baby. On Thursday he would not let his mother leave the room for some considerable time, standing at the door and blocking her when she tried to leave the room. Finally she thought it was all right to leave and did so, but Andy cried in great distress, with tears streaming down his face. As soon as I offered to get his mummy back into the room he stopped crying. While his mother had been there she told me that Andy was upset today because he had scraped his finger on the wall when he was on his tricycle. When she was telling me this he added, "I scraped my finger when I wasn't careful." Then another mishap arose when a little girl, Jeannie, had hit him on the head with a stick, after he had thrown leaves at her. He had then gone out and hit a little boy (passing it on, as it were). After he calmed down at this session, he played at washing Noddy, and at the end of the session he cried and struggled with his mother when she tried to put his coat on. Nothing was right for Andy that day, and I commiserated with him in the waiting room.

On Friday his mother brought back some toys that he had taken home from the Clinic on various occasions, but she said that he will not bring the doll back, so it looks as if Noddy's coming "alive" was a surprise indeed to him—he has kept one baby out of the way, only to have another come to life in front of his eyes. He occupied himself for most of the session washing the motor cars, then playing racing games with me. These games involved getting the cars filled with petrol very frequently, and this was usually followed almost immediately by a crash, both cars being pushed off the table.

WEEKLY REPORT NO. 14

SESSIONS 65 TO 68   *Age 2 years and 9 months*

There were only four sessions this week as I had, unfortunately, to cancel the last session of the week due to a family emergency. I asked that a message be given to Mrs. V. that due to these circumstances I would be unable to see Andy until further notice, but that I hoped to return within a few days and that I would contact her as soon as possible.

During the four sessions there was a similar pattern, with

a slight variation on the Thursday. This pattern consisted of his great initial unwillingness to come to the treatment room, followed by compliance when his mother accompanied him upstairs, then his allowing her to leave the room after a few minutes, quiet games during the session, and finally his unwillingness to leave the Clinic. The variation mentioned above was that on Thursday he came quite willingly upstairs at the beginning of the session, but otherwise the rest of the behavior was the same.

During sessions he played at the sink quite a lot, but did not seem to mind whether there was any water in it or not. He "washed" various toys, mostly the cars, saying that they must be nice and clean. There were car-crashing and aeroplane-flying games in which he invited me to join.

I saw Mr. V. this week, as Mrs. V. had said that he would be able to tell me more clearly about their difficulties. (These are omitted from this published report.) He also spoke with appreciation of the improvement in Andy, particularly in his sleeping habits. He spoke about the difficulties with his parents, particularly with his father. He was very pleased at his wife's agreeing to think about emigration at the end of Andy's treatment. He thinks it is a great advance that she will think about it even if they never actually go, as hitherto she has always said it would be impossible for her to leave her family so far behind. There is also another chance of a flat, more hopeful than the last one.

WEEKLY REPORT NO. 15

SESSIONS 69 TO 70

Following my return to work on Thursday, there were two sessions this week. He was very amiable at the beginning of the first session, but displaced his anger with me to a doll. He almost tore off the doll's knickers, ostensibly to look at "his" bum, but then screwed up his face and said "Poo-poos." He smacked the doll, saying that he would shake him. When

I interpreted his wish to shake me for not seeing him for such a long time, he attacked the doll with renewed vigor, then the teddy, saying that he would bash him. He put soap in his own mouth, and I said that he was really angry with me but is afraid to say so, so he takes it out on the doll and teddy instead, then washes his mouth out so that he will not say dirty, angry things to me. He then took up the doll and placed it on top of the teddy. I interpreted this as his wish for us to be together again, like daddy and mummy. He said, "Yiss, he smacks her and he bites her." He then wanted to sit on my lap to draw, which I took to be an expression of a more tender kind of loving feeling for me. I commented that I could see how he had missed me, but then (rather prematurely) I said that he wanted me to do to him what daddy does to mummy, being nice to mummy by smacking and biting; he threw the pencils on the floor, then a tumbler, which smashed. He became quite anxious at this, wanting to help me pick up the pieces. I said it was all right, and that I am all right too, for he hadn't really hurt me although he was angry with me. He then wanted to wee-wee, and returned to his session for the last few minutes accompanied by his mother. She said that Andy had missed me very much during the absence and that he had kept asking when he was coming back to see me, that he did not like being away.

On Monday of this week he had kept asking her whether I was with anybody. I said, for Andy's benefit, that he had thought I had left him and gone off to have fun with somebody else. Meanwhile he was lying on the couch with a very flushed face, very quiet, but when I added that he might even have thought that I would not come back at all, just as he used to be afraid his mummy might go off and not come back, he got up and yelled at me to shut up and held on to his mother.

The following day he was very difficult in the waiting room, declaring that he did not want to come with me. He ordered me and his mother about. Eventually when his mother brought him up to the treatment room, he would not let her go, even after he had said it was all right for her to go; he started crying, only stopping to tell me that he is going to have a dog and a puppy soon. I said once more that he had missed me when I was away. He asked me who I had been with, then answered himself, saying that he thought I was away with another friend. When I said that perhaps he meant another little boy, he became furious and started throwing everything in the room at me, except the couch and the lockers, and he did not throw those at me only because they were too heavy—he *tried* to lift the couch. I said that now he knows I'm really back he can let me know how annoyed he was. Although he continued throwing things at me, his aim had suddenly become much poorer and when it was time to leave he did not want to go out of the Clinic.

WEEKLY REPORT NO. 16

SESSIONS 71 TO 73

There were only three sessions this week, as his mother telephoned on Thursday to say that Andy had measles.

On each of the first three days of the week there was a repetition of the pattern of last Friday's session—difficulty in coming upstairs to the treatment room, crying at the beginning of the session, toy throwing, and finally reluctance to leave the Clinic. On Monday he greeted everyone he saw as "Mrs. Bum." When he started throwing things at me, I removed all the heavier articles out of reach, telling him that I knew he was angry with me, but I would not allow him to hurt me. He wanted to hurt me because he felt that *I* had hurt *him* by not seeing him. He played a game of dropping toys behind the couch, saying that they were poo-poos; then he climbed onto the window ledge, jumped down and climbed on the table; then he repeated the whole process. I commented that he thought it was very dangerous for me to go away from him, so he was doing dangerous things too, to make sure that I would look after him.

On Tuesday, Mrs. V. told me that they have a new flat and are hoping to move into it in a few weeks time. Grandfather said that he would not be able to look after Andy today, so she is unable to come to see me alone in the afternoon. Andy was looking unwell, with flushed face and running nose. When he cried I said that he was feeling unwell so he wanted to be with his mummy. He agreed that he wanted his mummy and we went downstairs to her, as I thought he needed her real presence. He went downstairs on his bottom. The next day he threw toys at me again. When I stopped him from doing this, he fell over and hit his head on the couch and started to cry. When I interpreted that his wish to hurt me had turned into a wish to hurt himself, because he was really quite fond of me as well as being angry with me, he stopped crying and swept all the toys out of the cupboard and kicked them around the room. I said that I thought he liked me, but he was angry with me, to which he replied, "I think I *don't* like you." I think this anger has more to do with my not stopping all the changes at home and not making him well; and because he was feeling so small and incapable of stopping the changes which were taking place. He was very amiable on leaving that day.

WEEKLY REPORT NO. 17

There were no sessions this week as Andy was still ill with measles. I sent him a "Get well" card.

WEEKLY REPORT NO. 18

SESSIONS 74 TO 77   *Age 2 years and 10 months*

Andy returned on Tuesday after his illness. He was looking very pale and thin. In the waiting room he stared at me when I entered, then said in a very hoarse voice, "I haven't seen you for a long time." When I agreed that it had been a long time and asked him whether he was better, he said, "No, I've got a bad cold already." When I said we could go upstairs and he could tell me all about it, he whispered very quietly, "I love you" and came up readily. When we were in the room he got out some cars, put them on the table, then wanted to climb up on my knee to play with them. I took him on my knee and he told me that he thought I was buried. I asked him what had made him think that and he said, "Because I thought you was dead." I said he must have been very sad and miserable to have been feeling not well and thinking that perhaps he might never see me again, especially with all the new things that had been happening (his mother had told me they were now in their new flat). I mentioned the new flat and said that I was sure they had taken all the things from their old house to the new place. We played a game of listing all the things he had taken with him —furniture, clothes, crockery, cutlery and so on. The things he listed were nearly all bedclothes. He told me that he is to get a puppy dog and ten pussies now that they are in their new flat.

The next day, however, he was not so keen to come upstairs, but when he did so we played at moving house, with the couch as the furniture van. He told me it had cost "six pounds and four bob" to move all the things and we again listed all the articles they had taken. When he had finished with the moving game, he looked at the pictures in a Rupert book, but the most fascinating picture to which he kept returning was of a fox with a large bushy tail. He named this animal correctly, but said "What's that" to everything else. When leaving he took the doll with him.

On the next two days he was very imperious with me and his mother, and I interpreted this as his wish to be able to have the say about where they are to live, that he wants to know that everybody is in the place where he wants them to be. He thereupon asked me when I was going on holiday, thinking it would be on Sunday morning. I said he must have heard his mummy say I would be going on holiday soon, but explained when it would be in such terms as I thought he would understand, emphasizing that I would be coming back and he would come to see me again. He said that he had been sick and I commiserated with him about this, saying what hard luck it is that he missed seeing me when he was sick and now I am going on holiday soon and he won't see me for another week. He started to talk "baby talk" and I said he must have felt miserable when he was a little baby when he did not see his mummy—perhaps he feels that if I think he is a little baby I won't go on holiday at all. Although the dogs in the garden next door had been barking for some time, he "heard" them for the first time when I made this interpretation and he leaned out of the window to see them, then ordered me about. I said that he was trying every way he knew to make me *not* go on holiday, at which he declared scornfully that I was a knick-knack bottom, wanted to go downstairs to his mummy, and kicked the picture book downstairs. The next day was a repetition of the imperious behavior, in which he was playing the man as a defense against his feeling helpless about my comings and goings. I again interpreted this in relation to the mother.

WEEKLY REPORT NO. 19

Sessions 78 to 81

There have been two main themes in Andy's play this week —the move to the new flat and being away from treatment. The first theme has been seen in the many "moving" games which he started last week, the main point being to reassure himself that nothing had been left behind. This included his grandparents, of course, particularly his grandfather, and he made several references to going to see him. This theme was closely linked with the idea of being away from me.

He spoke directly of my having been away on holiday

when in fact he had been ill and unable to come to treatment, but he also spoke at every session of the forthcoming holiday, mainly by remarking that I was not going on holiday the next day. I interpreted this as his anxiety as to whether we would see each other again after the holiday, just as he was anxious about seeing his grandfather again after moving to another house. He continued the throwing activities during the week, but was careful not actually to hit me with anything, although these activities were accompanied by many oaths and declarations of his dislike of me. I interpreted this ambivalence as a transference from his mother, from whom he found it particularly difficult to part at the beginning of sessions.

WEEKLY REPORT NO. 20

SESSIONS 82 TO 84

There was an unfortunate break in treatment this week, unfortunate in that it followed so soon after the Easter holiday. This break was caused by my being ill and unable to see Andy for the last two sessions.

On the first day of the week he was very cooperative about coming upstairs, running toward me as soon as he saw me and holding my hand on the way upstairs. During that session he was all smiles and played mostly with the trains, inviting me to join him. On the following two days there was a change, however, as he was able to express his annoyance at me for going on holiday and not seeing him.

On Tuesday he wanted to get something from the toy cupboard downstairs and chose a tin full of odd bits of plasticine. This he referred to as "cooking fat" and he used it variously as food, animals, transport, but principally as "throwing material." His mother told me later that at home when he plays at making meals he always includes cooking fat as one of the play items. This, she thinks, may derive from an accident when he was about eighteen months old: he spilled some cooking fat on his foot and was slightly burned. Since then she has always been very careful when he is near her at the stove and she warns him that there is cooking fat about. He asked me to make various animals from the plasticine and he would feed these animals with huge pieces much bigger than themselves, saying, "Poor pussy [doggy, moo-cow, etc.] is hungry, he hasn't had anything to eat for a long time." I related this to his own feeling of not being fed by me, taking it back to earlier feelings of not getting enough of mummy. Once he replied to this interpretation by saying, "Well, she's got me now," but the usual response was to tell me to shut up and then he would throw the plasticine about the room. When I also interpreted his feeding the animals as his wish to feed me, to see that I kept well, he offered me the plasticine to eat, inviting me to have some egg and chips.

WEEKLY REPORT NO. 21

Sessions 85 to 89   *Age 2 years and 11 months*

There have been many plasticine games this week, the usual routine being that he asked me to make some animal for him. That this represented our making babies together became clearer toward the end of the week when he named the two puppets "Shirley" and treated them as babies toward which he was very tender. Following this he asked me to make him a Shirley from plasticine. But to make babies was a dirty, aggressive business, as well as being exciting, for as soon as the animals were made he became excited, squashing them and finally thowing them and every other available piece of plasticine at the opposite wall. He would yell "Poo-poos" at the plasticine and call me "Mr. Bum," or threaten to hit me on the bleeding bum. This aggression had a quality totally different from that which followed on my interpretation, however. I interpreted his wish for us to make a baby together, just like mummy and daddy did, and he was furious. He yelled that he did not like me, that I was to shut up, that

he would hit me and so on. He was furious with disappointment at me and did not ask me to make any more animals.

This fury was different from that of previous weeks inasmuch as he showed a measure of control over his aggressive
impulses, partly through the defense of projection. This was
most clearly demonstrated in an incident following an interpretation of his wish that we should bite and smack each
other just like he thinks mummy and daddy do to each other
in bed at night. He yelled at me to shut up and he threatened
to kick me. At one time I would have had to hold him off
when he made such a threat, but on this occasion he stood
well away from me and made kicking movements at me. He
then leaned against the wall and slid down to the floor, end-
ing up with a bump. He glared at me and said, "*You* did
that." This was interpreted as his wish to hurt me, but at
the same time wishing to protect me from his anger, so he
says that I want to hurt him: at the same time he hurts himself (i.e., he completes the defensive maneuver by adding
turning against the self to projection).

His mother reported a situation about his sleeping difficulties which really arose from her own difficulties: she told
me originally that she used to leave her bedroom door open,
so that if Andy woke up during the night he came into their
bedroom and the tendency was for her to take him into
bed. I had recommended that she close her door and go to
Andy's room if he should wake up, emphasizing *her* right
to privacy and that this would be better for Andy. I made no
mention of her apparent need to have her privacy invaded
by him. She had told him she would be closing the door in
future and if he should want her during the night he should
call. In fact he has made no attempt to come into the parents'
bedroom since then and she *does* go to comfort him when he
wakes. She reported another incident which showed her difficulties and problems rather than Andy's, but one which she
seems to have handled well. She found him and a girl aged
four (a neighbor's child) engaged in a game of "doctors and

patients" which involved the girl "testing" him by feeling his penis. This spectacle filled her with horror, but nevertheless she was able to deal with it in a way which did not make Andy anxious and he was later able to talk about it to her. I could not show her that her horror had something to do with her own early experiences without going too deeply into it with her, but I pointed out the dangers of projecting her own attitudes onto children who are behaving in an age-adequate way in this kind of sexual curiosity.

WEEKLY REPORT NO. 22

SESSIONS 90 TO 94

The main theme this week seemed to be related to his efforts at coping with his aggression. There was no difficulty about his coming upstairs to sessions, but on the way up he played at being a pussy, miaowing all the time. Whenever I commented on this, he always said that the pussy bites. On Monday the cupboard door was hardly opened before he started throwing the contents at me. When I told him that he knew I did not like him to throw the heavy things at me he stopped, calling me a "stinky bum." For the rest of the session he played with the animals, mostly in a very controlling way, giving them orders before placing them in position, accompanying these orders with threats of punishment if they did not do what they were told. I interpreted this game as his wish to control the animals as he felt that I control him. I was again told that I was a "stinky bum."

The following day he carried the pussy game a step further by catching hold of my hand, miaowing and pretending to scratch me. He insisted on leaving the room to fetch his mummy when he had done this, but when she left after a few moments he cried bitterly. I showed him a puppet and he stopped crying immediately. He hit the puppet, telling it that he (the puppet) is a naughty boy who scratches and bites. I interpreted his unhappiness over his wishes to scratch and bite and throw things and his pretending that it is the puppet who does all these things. In the afternoon when I saw Mrs. V. she told me that Andy's sleep is particularly bad at the week ends at the moment. He frequently says to her that he *is* her little baby, her little darling. He plays much more on his own at home now, so that she can get on with her housework without too much of his hanging around. She expressed great relief at this, not least because she finds that she can be more patient with him when he does not make so many demands. She also spoke of her husband's new job, delivering tinned fruit to retailers in various towns. This job involves his being away from home on one night each week. Andy frequently asks her whether he should bring a tin of fruit to me, but he never actually does this.

At the following sessions he played with the animals, threatening to smack them if they were naughty. He showed me where his four-year-old cousin had bitten him on "the belly" (this was true: his mother said that the cousin had drawn blood). One day he started off the session by promising not to throw anything at me, and when he actually did throw something, I reminded him of his promise and he went back to using the animals as the objects of his aggression in play. He told me that he is using new trousers and promptly wanted to wee-wee—to try them out, as I said, for his mother has now adjusted all his trousers so that he can go to the toilet unaided. He demonstrated that he is perfectly capable of doing all that is necessary by himself and he was very pleased when I praised him for this achievement.

WEEKLY REPORT NO. 23

SESSIONS 95 TO 99

Andy deals with his anger with his father for being away from home so much by externalizing it, principally using cats. He played the pussy game going upstairs at the begin-

ning of the week, growling at me and miaowing. He projected his aggression onto them and then identified with
them, at the same time controlling them by making them
very small and carrying them about in a toy train. The link
with the feelings about the father was seen in a game in
which he drove a lorry to deliver tinned fruit, but instead
collected animals which growled and which he threatened
to smack for not doing what they were told, viz., to sit still
and not go away. This mechanism was confirmed by his
mother. She reported his fear of real cats and dogs and also
an incident in a self-service shop which was very crowded.
He does not like being among such crowds, and Mrs. V. told
him they would be there for only a few minutes. She turned
away to buy something and when she turned round again,
she saw Andy making faces and growling at the adults round
about.

When his anger with his father was interpreted, the pussy
game diminished, but he switched to another defensive
mechanism which consisted of his being the big person and
I the small. When I said that he made me into a small person
so that he could tell me what to do and so that he need not
be frightened of me, he caressed me and called me his little
daddy. The following day he made me even smaller by saying that he is a big boy and I am a little girl. In this role
play he took me shopping, but he changed his mind and
instead we went to a clinic because he was ill (clutching his
penis). When I asked what was wrong he said that he had a
bad cough and that I should test his back. Then he suddenly
changed his mind and said that he should test *my* back. He
was very insistent about this and became quite excited, push-
ing me toward the couch with one hand and clutching at
his penis with the other. I remarked that he was really thinking of us making a baby together, at which he said that *I* was
the babba and that he is my mummy. The excitement
reached the usual climax when he wanted to wee-wee. The
anger with the father for being away is not unassociated with

the fantasy that when the father is out of the way, he and mummy can make babbas together.

WEEKLY REPORT NO. 24

SESSIONS 100 TO 104

Sessions this week have followed a well-defined pattern which seems to concern his "choice" of identifications. Hitherto there has been a marked freedom of identifications with both mother and mather, but more and more he identifies with father, particularly in his role as authority figure. Occasionally, however, there appears to be some confusion, for while he assumes the *role* of father in his games with me, his *behavior* is motherly. An interesting point about these games now is that instead of saying, "You be the mother, baby, father, etc., and I'll be the daddy, mummy, etc.," he now addresses me directly as "daddy, mummy, babba, little girl, nana, grandpa," etc. The state of the transference is thus made very clear for me to understand. When he addresses me as "friend," then I am a real, nontransference person for him.

Games have varied between those with trains and lorries where he is always the daddy and I am a babba whom he takes for a run or takes shopping, and those games in which we both look after dolls (babbas). He is usually very tender with the babbas, wanting them to have a good view from the lorry, wanting them well wrapped up in case they should catch cold and so on, but occasionally he scolds them for being naughty. Their naughtiness is always anal—they wet themselves, do poo-poos, get themselves dirty and so on, and he hastens to clean them. It is on such occasions that although he says he is daddy, he really mothers the babies.

Outside sessions he has taken to addressing everybody he meets, male and female, as "Mrs. Bum," his reasoning for this mode of address being that as everybody has a bum, then they are all called Mrs. Bum. When I asked why he did not call men Mr. Bum, he said, "Because they're Mrs. Bum."

WEEKLY REPORT NO. 25

SESSIONS 105 TO 109

Sessions this week were characterized by his uniform friendliness toward me. He came eagerly upstairs for his sessions; there were no "difficult" scenes either in the waiting room or on the stairs. During sessions he played with the trains mostly, giving the dolls and the animals rides—usually to Hereford (I have been unable to discover why Hereford is always chosen; his mother reports that he uses the same town for the same purpose at home, but she does not know how he could have got hold of the name); making animals out of plasticine. I saw this in association with his birthday being on Friday, and possibly that he was keeping in my good books for present purposes (perhaps he has been threatened by parents or grandparents that he would not receive birthday presents if he is naughty).

Friday morning saw the breakdown of this unnaturally good behavior. He greeted me with a smile in the waiting room, but when we got outside he sat on the bottom step and looked at me. I wished him many happy returns and he acknowledged this by saying that he is a big boy now. He got up and we went upstairs. I asked him what presents he had had and he told me his grandpa had given him a garage. When we were in the treatment room, I asked what his daddy and mummy had given him. He scowled and said "Nothing." It transpired that he and his mummy were going later to choose a lorry for him. When I asked whether he had thought I would have a present for him, he scowled again and told me to shut up, but when I asked what he would have liked from me, he said, "An eggie-train" (I had given him a little cardboard train with Easter eggs on it at Eastertime). When I sympathized with his disappointment at not having a present from me on his birthday, he again told me to shut up and was very aggressive during the rest of the session. He constantly interrupted anything I started to say, and this continued until we went down to the waiting room together, his parting words being that he did not like me.

WEEKLY REPORT NO. 26

SESSIONS 110 TO 112   *Age 3 years*

There were only three sessions this week as it included the Whitsun holiday. He was very eager to come up to his sessions on Wednesday and Thursday, in marked contrast to his behavior on Friday. During the first two sessions, he was very amiable, playing quietly, including me in all his games and anticipating many of my usual remarks which occur in the course of our meetings, e.g., when he hears a noise and asks me what it is, I ask him what he thinks it is; on Wednesday and Thursday when he heard a noise he said, "What's that? What do you think it is?" The games themselves were almost exclusively with the train, which he loaded with pieces of plasticine. He occasionally said that the plasticine is poo-poos and laughed.

On Friday, however, he did not want to come upstairs with me, but eventually he did so when I said that I would go upstairs and he could come up with his mummy. He said that she was not to come up, but was to stay there. Nevertheless, when I started to leave the room, he insisted on her coming with us. She accompanied us to the treatment room and left in a few minutes. He was very negative toward me during the whole session, telling me to shut up, no matter what I said, telling me he did not like me. I associated this behavior with that of the previous Friday and saw it in terms of his disappointment in me on two counts—my not giving him a birthday present and my not seeing him at the week end. I saw this as a transference feeling from the father whose new job entails his being away from home overnight on one night a week (but this means in fact that Andy does not see him for about thirty-six hours). To Andy, father's going away like this means that he does not like Andy, just as my not seeing him and my not giving him a present mean the same thing. He naturally does not like me in return, but denies the same feeling toward his father. I interpreted his feeling that I did not like him, but assured him that not giving a present and not seeing him at week ends do not mean this. This interpretation has no meaning for him, I think, for he is still at the stage where love must be proved by gifts. After discussion with my supervisor, we decided to wait and see how this reaction develops and to have an actual gift as a stand-by if his inability to accept the interpretation is confirmed by further material.

WEEKLY REPORT NO. 27

Sessions 113 to 116

Mrs. V. telephoned on Monday morning to ask whether it would be all right if she did not bring Andy that morning, because she had a chance of renting a house with a garden and had to go along to the factor's office at 10:30 to see about it. She wondered whether it would be possible to bring him later in the day. It was not possible for me to see him later, but I said that she should not miss this chance of getting such a house and that I would see them at the usual time on Tuesday.

When I saw Mrs. V. on Tuesday for her weekly interview, she told me she had really gone to the factor's office to please her mother-in-law. The possible house is very near the grandparents' home, but Mrs. V. knew that her chances of getting it were very slender—in fact, they turned out to be non-existent as the owners had decided to sell the house rather than to let it for rent. She reported that Andy's sleeping continues to be very good and that altogether life with him is very pleasant. The rest of this interview concerned her views of her husband's continued dependence on his parents.

Sessions with Andy contained material similar to that of

previous weeks, during which he has played with the trains, calling them lorries, and he has taken dolls, teddy bears and me for rides in his lorry to Hereford. He is very much identified with his father in this activity, saying that he (Andy) is the daddy and we (the dolls and I) are his babies. He often lies down on the couch during these games, screwing up his face and saying that daddy has a bad head, he has hurt his head on the lorry, he has crashed his lorry and isn't feeling well. The reality basis of this identification was reported by his mother: the father has not had any accidents, but frequently when he comes home in the evening he complains of tiredness and headache and lies down before supper. At such times she tells Andy to be quiet as daddy wants to rest his sore head. Andy always is quiet at such times and often asks his daddy whether his head is better. I interpreted his concern about his daddy's sore head, saying that he might be worried about it because he did not like his daddy to be away from home. His response was to tell me to shut up and the next morning he told his mother he did not want to come to see his friend.

WEEKLY REPORT NO. 28

SESSIONS 117 TO 121

There has been little new of note in the material this week; Andy's games and fantasies show his continuing wish to be the daddy, going off on his lorry to work and taking his babbas with him for a good time. Interpretation of these games has been widened from merely being a verbalization of his wish to be big like his daddy, to include his wish that his daddy would take *him* with him on the lorry to give him a good time and that he tries to bring this about by showing that if he were the daddy he would be very nice to his babbas. His response to this repeated interpretation was to ask me why his daddy goes to work, does everybody go to work, do I go to work? I asked him whether he had asked his mummy and his daddy all these questions and what they said about it. He said that he had not asked them, but the following day reported that his daddy went to get money, to buy things for Andy.

Mrs. V. had little to report in her interview, except that Andy's sleeping is now all that she could wish and has been so for about four or five weeks. I took the opportunity of clarifying some points in the history about which my information had not been very clear, particularly about feeding. I learned that when Andy was admitted to the hospital at the age of three weeks he had been put on the bottle immediately. Some weeks later, when his condition was considered to be very grave and his weight was down to about 5 pounds, he was put on a continuous plasma drip. This treatment was instigated by a new doctor in the children's ward and from this point Andy progressed rapidly. She was not officially allowed to be near him while he was in the hospital, but one of the Sisters used to let her feed him about once a week and sometimes she was allowed to sit by his bed and hold him. He became a fat baby when he came home from the hospital. When he was eight months old the local Child Welfare Clinic said he ought to start on solids and she put him on baby food. However, he immediately developed diarrhea and as she was very concerned lest this was the start of another bout of gastroenteritis, she telephoned the nice Sister in the hospital who had told her to do so if she were ever concerned about the child. The doctor who had attended him told her to put him back on the bottle again and not to worry about solids at the moment; since he was progressing satisfactorily on a liquid diet, there was no need to change it just because of his age. This doctor also contacted the Child Welfare Clinic and told them this also. Andy continued to thrive, except that whenever she tried him on solids again he got diarrhea, and in fact it was not until he was almost two years old that he was able to "keep" solids. Since then there has been no difficulty. He has no food fads and has a very good appetite. I asked her whether he was given the opportunity of biting things, e.g., a teething ring, as he was not biting biscuits and so on, but she said that she could not really remember anything special about his biting then, although he soon developed the habit of biting towels, facecloths, etc., when being bathed.

At the end of the interview she remembered to tell me that the family are going on holiday for a week, starting a week from now. This is the only date this summer on which her husband can get away. The paternal grandparents are going with them.

WEEKLY REPORT NO. 29

Sessions 122 to 126

The material this week has again been centered on his feelings about his father being away every day to work and away for one night each week. This has been brought much more acutely into the transference because of the impending holiday. His games have included not only those familiar ones of reversing roles (he becomes the one who goes away instead of the one who is left), but also hiding games in which he is quickly found.

Interpretation of the hiding games was along the lines that he is afraid that when he goes away on holiday I may not be here on his return, I may get lost, so he plays at hiding and finding to make sure that we will find each other again. This fear was related to his anxiety when his daddy goes away, and in general terms about his fear of losing his mummy also. The response to this interpretation was a gradual association of aggression with the hiding games. He took toys from the locker and hid them behind the couch, searched for them and of course found them. He would greet their finding with a cry of triumph: "Here you are!" This was quickly followed with an angry growl at them and then their being thrown violently against the wall. This anger was interpreted as being directed against those who go away from him and make him feel anxious, at first me for not going on holiday with him, later daddy for going to work, then mummy for not being with him all the time when he was a little baby. He was most insistent that I should come with him to the seashore, directly angry when I said that I could not, but that he could take me with him in his mind: he could remember me even if he could not see me (his mother had reported on Tuesday that on week ends now he talks about me and coming to see me on Monday, i.e., object constancy is in the process of establishment). He then seemed to accept that I could not come with him, because *"you* go to work too."

WEEKLY REPORT NO. 30

Age 3 years and 1 month

There were no sessions this week as the family had gone on holiday for a week.

WEEKLY REPORT NO. 31

SESSIONS 127 TO 131

Andy returned this week from a holiday by the seaside with his parents and grandparents. He was full of "sand games" and for a while the lorry which he so often rides and drives in sessions was replaced by a donkey.

He greeted me belligerently in the waiting room on the first day by asking me where I had been, had I been to the seaside too? During the session he repeated this in various versions, putting on a show of anger with me for not being with him on holiday. This I took to express both a wish that I had been with him, but also to ward off *my* possible anger for his deserting me, by a reversal. On interpretation of this, he hotly denied that he had wanted me to be with him and struck me on the arm, saying that he was fed up, but shortly afterward he came up to me and leaned his head against my arm and asked me who had been with me when I went on holiday. When I asked, "If I had been on holiday, who do you think would have been with me?" he muttered, "Another friend." I interpreted this to mean that he wanted me all to himself, just as he really wants his mummy and daddy all to himself and not to share them with another little boy or girl. This angered him and he vowed that he would "do" me if I didn't shut up. The thought of a sibling always angers him, although he manages to dissimulate when he is in the presence of babies; e.g., he makes a great show of loving his girl cousin.

Mrs. V. told me that the holiday had been a great success as far as Andy was concerned and that the grandparents had been very "good," i.e., they had not interfered too much. Indeed, she emphasized how fond they are of him. He had asked for me on several occasions, especially whether I would later come to the seaside place with him. On the Sunday before returning to treatment he had mentioned to a visitor that he was going to see his friend the next day to tell him all about the donkeys. For the remaining sessions of the week he played the games mentioned, but on Thursday and Friday he reverted to his favorite lorry, although there seemed to be a frantic air about the journeys he was constantly making on his lorry, with the emphasis on the return home at the end of the journey. I took this to refer to his anxiety about his father's return home from work, primarily arising from his ambivalence toward the father and his frequent absences.

WEEKLY REPORT NO. 32

SESSIONS 132 TO 136

The emphasis once again this week has been on the lorry games, but mostly he plays at taking me for a ride with him when he goes on a journey, i.e., he is the adult driver and I am the child passenger. This is a frequently used mechanism: reversal of roles in aid of wish fulfillment; and it is a transference phenomenon indicating his solution to the problem of his father's going away.

Mrs. V. confirmed his anxiety about the father's absences, saying that he often asks when daddy will be home, sometimes in such a way as to make it clear that he wonders whether daddy will ever return. On one occasion last week he asked whether his daddy would be home in the morning when he woke up. As this was one of the times when Mr. V. was away overnight, Mrs. V. told him that daddy would not be back until after lunchtime the following day. However, as soon as he woke up the following morning he came rushing into her bedroom calling for his daddy, and when she told him daddy would not be back until later that day (as she had already told him) he burst into tears. It does not seem to be disturbing his sleeping, however, for he remains asleep in his own room every night. Occasionally he awakes about 6:30 A.M. and then comes into the parents' bedroom. At such times Mrs. V. takes him into bed and he falls asleep again for another hour or so. She has noticed that he does not do this when his father is not at home.

There are other manifestations of his wish to control the adults' behavior by making them into the small ones while he becomes the big one. He calls me "Janet" and describes me as a little girl; he wants me to go to the doctor (him) to be examined or treated; this consists of listening through an imaginary stethoscope held to my chest. These activities are interpreted as his wish to be able to make the grownups do what he would like, because sometimes he feels that they pay no attention to his wishes because he is small, and this upsets him as well as making him angry. The usual response to such interpretations is for him to ignore me completely or to say "What?" again and again. The response is further interpreted as his not wanting to hear what I say, because it makes him unhappy. This usually provokes further "Janet" games, i.e., further attempts to deny his position as a child vis-à-vis the adults.

WEEKLY REPORT NO. 33

Sessions 137 to 141

I have spent some time this week in preparing him for the forthcoming. holiday and have told his mother that I am doing so. His early responses were to ignore whatever I said on this subject; later he became angry whenever it was mentioned, and at the end of the week he was asking me whether the toys would have a good time while *he* was going on holiday.

The lorry games have persisted to some extent, although the frantic air has largely disappeared and he seems to be deriving actual pleasure from the identification with father, rather than using the games as an expression of anxiety and a defense against it.

Mrs. V. reported that his only mention of the forthcoming holiday has been to ask whether they are going back to the same seaside place as before. She has told him that they would not be going away for so long, but has promised him visits to the zoo, the river and so on. She also reports a lessening of anxiety about his father's return, but an increase of the number of visits he is making to his grandparents at his own request. She repeated that he does not really care for his grandmother, but is very fond of his grandfather.

In the transference I am still the father who is controlled by the reversal of roles and he treats me as he himself would like to be treated by his father.

WEEKLY REPORT NO. 34

Sessions 142 to 145   *Age 3 years and 2 months*

During this last week before the long summer break he has tried to postpone the parting in two ways: at first, he did this directly by trying to prolong each session and finally when he was left with his mother in the waiting room he would not put on his coat to go home; secondly, when I have mentioned the holiday and at the same time spoken of the time when he would be coming back to see me, he invariably responded by saying simply, "I'll see you tomorrow." This was interpreted as his wish for us not to part, and so long as he could say that he would see me the following day (and I did not contradict this) he could feel that perhaps I would not go away after all. The response to this was a repetition of the abuse he used to heap on me earlier in the treatment—I was a stinking bum, etc., and this was interpreted as a transference feeling associated with partings from his daddy, and earlier from his mummy. This in turn produced more abuse and I told him that I knew how angry he must feel and must have felt at being left, but no matter how angry he was with me, he would not really hurt me, because he also loved me.

Mrs. V. was not looking forward to the holiday very much as it would mean more time with the grandparents. I tried to point out that since they did not now live in the same house, she had a choice about the number of visits she made to them. However, she rationalized this by saying that it was convenient for her to do so, since Andy is sometimes a nuisance when she goes shopping and she can leave him with the grandparents at those times. She seemed quite relieved when I added that anyway he likes visiting them, and it transpired that she thought I would disapprove of his going to see them too often.

WEEKLY REPORT NO. 35

SESSIONS 146 TO 147   *Age 3 years and 3 months*

There were only two sessions this week. Mrs. V. telephoned on Monday to say that she would not be coming to the Clinic that day. When I spoke to her she sounded tearful and said that she had had a shock about something her husband had been doing; she did not want to come to the Clinic for fear she might cry in the waiting room. She would not tell me what it was and even when I offered to give her an appointment on her own she would not accept, for fear of breaking down in my presence. However, she agreed to telephone me the following day. Andy was in the telephone box with her and he said hello to me, telling me he would see me tomorrow.

On the following day Mrs. V. telephoned me and said she felt a bit better and agreed to come and see me, without Andy, on the Wednesday. On Wednesday she told me about the "shock." She had found that her husband was becoming increasingly morose and depressed during the holiday and had asked him what was troubling him. At first he complained about the flat and how infrequently they managed to get out now that they are living away from his parents, but later he confessed that he had been flirting with another woman. Mrs. V. had been flabbergasted at this news; it was so unlike her husband and she had been very upset for days. She had heard of this kind of thing happening to others, but it never dawned on her that it could happen to her and "her Andy" (she added, "Big Andy, I mean"). She was now getting over it, accepting it as "one of those things" and realized that the actual affair had not amounted to much. She thought that his behavior was due to his depression and not the other way about. I offered to see Mr. V. to find out whether there was any way in which I could help in the situation and together we tried to find a formula which would enable Mr. V. to come and see me without feeling that I was putting him on the carpet. It was finally decided that she should say that I had mentioned that Mr. V. had not been to see me for some time, although we had arranged at the beginning of Andy's treatment that he *would* come from time to time.

Andy came for sessions on Thursday and Friday. He found great difficulty in separating from his mother before sessions and all through the sessions he wanted to go back downstairs. I curtailed both sessions because of his anxiety. Interpretation was limited to saying that he was afraid his mummy might go away from him in the way that I had done during the holiday. There were obviously many factors involved in the anxiety, but I felt that he was in no state to accept analysis of them, but that there would be plenty of time later to deal with it.

WEEKLY REPORT NO. 36

Sessions 148 to 152

Mr. V. has not yet accepted my invitation to come and see me. He told his wife that he would like to come but he cannot do so because his shift would not permit it. He is giving up his present job at the end of this week, so he could come and see me next week.

Mrs. V. was able to tell me more about Andy during the holidays. He had enjoyed all their outings to the seaside, the zoo, and Richmond Park. His sleep had been good until the last two weeks when he had been waking up frequently and calling for her and his daddy. He had asked often when he was going to see his friend again and had been quickly reassured when she had said "in so many weeks or days." When I commented that his sleep disturbance was not surprising when one considered the upset there had been between his parents, she declared he could not know anything about it for they had both been very careful not to let him know. I said this would be impossible and at the very least he knew that she was upset because of something his daddy had done: I reminded her that he had been present when she told me this on the telephone last week. She grimaced and said that she had forgotten this and probably he really knew quite a bit about it. She remembered another occasion on which he must have heard it being discussed between her and his grandparents. His grandmother had implied that either the story was untrue or it was Mrs. V.'s fault. She had been very angry at this and there had been a row. Nevertheless, there is now talk of them going back to live at the grandparents' house. Mr. V. says this would be better because their present flat is too expensive, particularly since he will be out of work at the end of this week, but Mrs. V. thinks that it is because her husband has never really settled down to marriage— "he's so young in some ways"—and that he is really depressed when it is necessary to stay in during the evenings so much, because of Andy. She does not like the idea of moving back, but somewhere is the idea that she must comply with this if the marriage is to be kept together. I said I did not think moving back would be a very good idea for Andy, but she should try to get her husband to come to see me before they made any move.

During sessions Andy has been very restless. He would not settle down to anything for any length of time but went from one occupation to another rapidly. I interpreted this restlessness as being like his uncertainty about where he is going to live and about what is happening at home between his mummy and daddy. This produced a combination of denial and increased pointless activity, and I remarked that it must seem to him that he cannot depend on anybody staying in the place they usually stay in, e.g., I go off on long holidays. He called me a "stinky bum"; nevertheless, toward the end of the week he was quieter, and on Friday he even started to play building games in which I was to cooperate, e.g., building garages for cars. He demolished the garages as soon as they were built and then demanded that I rebuild them. I interpreted this game as his way of telling me that he felt responsible for all the upsets at home and asking me to make sure that the damage he caused was not permanent and could be put right. He replied, "You *can* make the garages all right, friend, can't you?"

Comment

His anxiety about the reality situation and his guilt about it are seen in this week's sessions. There seems little that I can do at the moment except to try to deal with the anxiety by helping him to verbalize it and for me to accept the role of "reconstructor" until the reality situation settles down. It is interesting that the sleep disturbance makes its reappearance now, although it takes the form of waking up rather than in difficulty in getting to sleep.

WEEKLY REPORT NO. 37

SESSIONS 153 TO 157   *Age 3 years and 4 months*

Andy's father had arranged to see me on Wednesday, but at the last moment Mrs. V. telephoned to say he would be unable to come as he had to go to an appointment for a job. She told me that they have decided to go back to live with her in-laws and she feels this to be the best solution of the situation. She would prefer to be in a home of her own, but realizes that her husband is not happy and she is therefore prepared to put up with the inconvenience of the move. She says that she must make it perfectly clear to her in-laws that they must not interfere with the upbringing of Andy. His sleeping is not too bad at the moment. She commented again on his ability to play by himself.

During sessions his play has been much more coherent than recently, i.e., he does not dash about from one activity to another. His favorite game continues to be the building of garages, although sometimes he also wants me to make "roads" for the cars out of flattened pieces of plasticine. He does not demolish the garages as he did last week, but expresses dissatisfaction with everything I make, saying, "That's too big, too small, too wide" and so on. I interpreted this dissatisfaction as relating to his annoyance with his daddy and mummy and that it was also his narking at me in the way they narked at him. This got a mixed reception—first an indignation accompanied by spitting, then an indulgent "you are a silly thing" accompanied by a grin. Shortly afterward he called me "Mummy" and immediately looked sharply at me, saying, "Aren't I a silly thing, I got you all mixed up, friend." At subsequent sessions he started to involve me in racing games which were always friendly, and he announced the result of each race *before* it was run. I commented that he felt that if he were in charge, everything would go just the way he wanted, instead of all higgledy-piggledy. He grinned and said, "Yes, that's right, darling" and announced the result of the next race.

WEEKLY REPORT NO. 38

Sessions 158 to 162

Andy and his parents have moved out of their own flat and have now gone back to live with Mr. V.'s parents. The only hint of this (and I did not understand it at the time) in Andy's talk and behavior was during the Tuesday session, when he asked me whether I would like to come and play in his garden. Although I knew that they did not have a garden in their flat, I did not make the connection that he was now living in a house which does have one. I thought that he meant the park near his home, so I took up his wish to play with me outside his session time. This has become a central theme at the moment and takes various forms, e.g., direct wishes to meet me outside; stimulating my curiosity about his extra-Clinic activities by telling me a little about them and then leaving the subject in mid air ("I went to see George yesterday . . . you be like the little girl I played with yesterday . . . etc.); asking me questions about my life outside the Clinic. I saw this material as related to extending our relationship beyond the frustrating limits of fifty minutes a day, and also to his extending his activities among his age peers.

Mr. V. came to see me this week, and it was he who told me about the family move. This move has been rationalized by him as being due to financial necessity caused by his giving up his last job. I did not follow this up by remarking that it was he who produced this necessity by giving up the job before he had another to go to, which has not been his practice in the past. However, I did say that I thought this was a move which would have to be carefully watched from the angle of its effect on Andy, particularly as far as it might affect him by presenting to him contradictory attitudes between his parents and grandparents. He said that he had taken good care of this by having a serious talk with his parents before they moved back into their house. He was very firm with them, telling them that on no account were they to interfere with Andy's upbringing. He thinks they will pay attention to this, and seemed to be quite convinced of it even when I said that they had not done so in the past. I felt he was very relieved that I did not take up with him the reasons for his giving up his job. In fact, I concentrated on enlisting his support in Andy's treatment, stressing the importance of the father to a child at his level of development and the contribution the father can make. He was enthusiastic about the idea that I would help him to understand what is going on and indeed verbalized the unconscious meaning (that I am his "good" father) when telling me that *his* father was of no help to him when he was young and that he might have to learn how to help Andy, as he had had no previous experience of a good relationship between a father and son.

Although Andy seemed to give me no further information about the move, I interpreted this absence of information as his response to my not giving him any information about my life outside the Clinic. He responded to this interpretation by an increase in his direct curiosity about me: "Have you got a little girl, boy, dog, cat, hamster, budgie? Where is your house? Where is your car? Have you got a daddy, mummy, nana, granda?" I replied to all these questions by returning them to him in the form, "Do you think I have a . . . ?" He invariably replied, "No, you haven't"; when I took this further by saying that I thought he wanted me just to have a little Andy and nobody else, he sometimes responded by saying "Yes," but at the end of the week he said, without apparent resentment but with some regret, that I *could* have a little boy, i.e., he reluctantly gives me permission to have one.

He told me about his two hamsters. It is remarkable how little he speaks of these, although I understand from his mother that he is very fond of them. I suppose these are the little boys and so on that he does not tell me about in case I should be jealous of them.

Comment

I am not happy about the effect of this move back to the grandparents' house, but it seems to have been brought about by the father's need to be near them. I think Mrs. V. will be better able to cope with the situation now than she was before treatment started; at least she can now acknowledge and allow the grandparents' fondness for Andy and see that it is not altogether a pernicious influence on him. Andy seems to be beginning to see me as not just his "friend," nor just as a transference object, but as a separate individual, i.e., this may be the beginning of a social sense in a way.

WEEKLY REPORT NO. 39

SESSIONS 163 TO 167

On Monday he started playing an old game of his, the "doctor-patient" game, in which he invited me to lie down on the couch so that he could "test" me, i.e., listen to my chest. In addition to listening, he also wanted to feel my tummy. I took from this game the meaning that he reverses the roles and that he has been unwell, and that the reversal acts as a means of countering his anxiety about being examined. However, the only information I could get from him was that he had a sore leg, which he alleged had bumped against a chair. I interpreted his fear of being examined as being a fear that the doctor would do something bad to him, but this was met with a denial and a repeated wish for me to lie down. When I said that we could pretend that he was the doctor and I the patient and he would tell me what he is going to do to me, he responded by telling me that I had a sore tummy and that he would have to cut off my leg (and at this point he started to "saw" at my leg and then punched my leg as hard as he could). I said that it seemed that he was afraid that the doctor would cut off his winkie, just as he had been afraid of this when he went to see a doctor before. He replied that the doctor wouldn't cut off his winkie, he would cut hers off.

The same game was his principal interest on the following day, and I continued to interpret his interest in it as his way of controlling his castration fear, but with the addition that he was afraid that his mummy's winkie had been cut off and that the same thing would happen to him. His denial of this included the very firm assertion that his mummy's winkie had *not* been cut off, but that she still had one. I said that he knew very well that his mummy had no winkie, that he thought therefore that she had lost it, but the fact is that mummies have never had winkies at all. When he asked what they have instead, I said that some children I know call what mummies have "baby holes." He accepted this name without evincing further interest in why this particular name should be used.

In my interview with the mother I learned why the "doctor" game had been so predominant. Andy had in fact knocked his leg against a chair and on the same evening he had complained of a pain at the back of his thigh when he got up from the floor. His mother had immediately thought he might have ruptured himself! Her husband had said that she was being silly, and pointed out the obvious, that the back of the thigh is not the usual site of a rupture, but she had taken it that children are unreliable about localizing the site of a pain and he *had* hit himself in the groin. She took

Andy to the doctor (a woman), who had examined Andy's abdomen and genitals to check whether or not he was ruptured. Since then he had been wanting to "test" everybody in the house. We discussed this incident from the point of view of her own anxiety about him and how the early experience of his going to the hospital and having been so ill had rather complicated her attitude to him, i.e., the anxiety about his real state of health at that time had made her react too strongly to later accidents and illnesses. She acknowledged the truth of this, but added that she did not seem to be able to help herself, she just had to take him to a doctor when there is the slightest possibility of there being anything wrong with him. I said I thought we ought to do some work on this together because it would help her as well as Andy. Such examinations made him anxious and should be avoided unless they were really necessary.

Later in the week Andy dropped the doctor game in favor of getting me to be a puppet which he could tell what to do and to whom he gave surprise presents. This was another reversal, of course, but this time he was showing me how reversal is used for positive rather than negative ends, i.e., the nice things he would like the adults to do for him. I also saw it as another aspect of his castration complex: if adults, especially the mother, can take away his penis, they can also give him a bigger and better one. When I interpreted this, he made the apparent *non sequitur* that "Ladies have bums and baby holes, they don't have winkies." It emerged that this covered the fantasy that his mummy had had a winkie, but that she had given it to him when he was a little baby, i.e., this fantasy denies the opposite one that she might take it away.

WEEKLY REPORT NO. 40

Sessions 168 to 172

Mr. V. came this week and we made the arrangement that he and his wife should alternate in their weekly interview with me. He was pleased at the idea because he felt he would be able to give me a different picture of Andy. He feels his wife is too anxious about Andy's health and although he does not blame her, he does get irritated about it and he feels she should try harder to control her anxiety. As I had recently heard indirectly that Mr. V.'s mother had lost two children in infancy and that she blamed the doctors for not saving their lives, I spoke about the anxieties of mothers during the illness of their children. Mr. V. recognized that an important cause of his wife's anxiety was Andy's real early illness, but he thought that there must be something else in it. He thought this because he himself had been seriously ill as a child and had been in the hospital for six months, not very long after an older sister had died. He felt that his mother's attitude had been unnatural: one would have thought that she would have been anxious about him after that, but on the contrary, she always seemed to be out at work and he and his sister were left alone a good deal. He sees his mother and his wife as two opposite types, neither of whom could hit on the happy medium in looking after their children, one not concerned enough, the other *too* concerned. This information throws much light on Mr. V.'s inability to leave his mother, but I did not explore this with him, preferring to talk in terms of how the parents' attitudes could affect Andy, particularly in increasing his anxiety about the integrity of his body.

WEEKLY REPORT NO. 41

SESSIONS 173 TO 178   *Age 3 years and 5 months*

Andy's "grown-up" games continued with unabated enthusiasm. In these games we built garages, castles, and houses; we directed the traffic and looked after the animals in the zoo. Sometimes we were age-equals, but at other times he was the grownup and I was the "darling" child who was taken around by him to see the zoo, the park; I was shown how people cross the road, how they cook, how they shop, how they drive buses and lorries. He seemed to be passing on all the information he had ready at his disposal. But mainly I got the impression that he was using me as a substitute for somebody of his own age.

I took this up with Mrs. V. as indicating his readiness for nursery school and his need to extend his range in learning in a group of children. She was very eager about the idea and in fact she 'had already made some inquiries about schools. I spoke to Mrs. V. of the possibility of termination of treatment, or at least reduction in the number of sessions, at the end of this term. She had had the idea that as Andy is much better now, I would probably be finishing treatment then— hence the inquiries about nursery schools. There appears to be no suitable school near their home, but she had enlisted the help of the Health Visitor in inquiring about more distant ones.

Andy was very curious about what his daddy had said to me and what I had said to him. I had told Mr. V. that he should make a point of telling Andy that he had been to see me, in this way assuring him of his father's interest in him. He wanted to know whether I had gone in his daddy's motorcycle and whether we had gone in my car. I interpreted this as his wondering whether his daddy would take his place with me because of his own wish to take his daddy's place— a theme which had again appeared in his play this week.

Another factor, of course, in his playing at being the grownup was his desire to progress. He was very much the little boy who puts the baby things behind him; e.g., at the end of sessions he would say, "We'd better wash our hands now." On previous occasions when washing his hands, this soon became a splashing, messy game, but now he really was washing and drying them in a businesslike way. He also insisted on my staying in the room when he wanted to go to the lavatory. Whenever we met anybody on the stairs, he stood aside to let them pass, but always turned to me afterwards, saying, "I let that Mrs. pass, didn't I?" I always said that I had seen him and I complimented him on his good manners; on one occasion he replied, *"Sometimes* I'm quite good, aren't I?"

WEEKLY REPORT NO. 42

SESSIONS 179 TO 183

Mr. V. could not come this week so Mrs. V. came instead. She had thought that Andy was going to be ill this week end, but it had turned out to be only a slight cold. He had been coughing through the night and could not sleep. She did not insist on his lying in his own bed, but had made up a bed on two armchairs for him in her bedroom and he had eventually gone to sleep there. The following night she had offered to do the same as she thought his cough was still as bad, but Andy had insisted on sleeping in his own room, saying that his cough was better. In fact, he then slept the whole night in his own room. I congratulated both of them—Mrs. V. on her flexibility in handling the situation and Andy on knowing when he would feel better sleeping near her and yet being able the following night to go back to sleeping on his own. I thought this a very clear example of his object constancy.

His imaginative play has also taken on a more mature coloring. Instead of the repetitive activities and the acting out of so much of his previous play, his games now have a story line, constructed as we go along. Although these games naturally have a fantasy content, they tend to be more sublimatory in character. A typical favorite is the cowboys-and-Red-Indians game. We construct a town of plasticine inhabited by various cowboys, including a chief cowboy. There is also a tribe of Indians, including a chief Indian. There is a fight and several cowboys and Indians bite the dust, but never the chiefs. Eventually the chiefs decide that there has been enough fighting, the dead ones are revived and everybody comes into the town, the Indians are given houses and everybody has a party and becomes friends. Fighting usually breaks out again and the same conclusion is reached. This game is not an anxiety-driven one, but seems to me to represent his acceptance of his own aggression, including the possibilities of reparation.

WEEKLY REPORT NO. 43

SESSIONS 184 TO 188

Andy has gone back to a form of "waiting-room behavior" which was prominent in an earlier phase of his treatment, viz., reluctance to come with me to the consulting room, dilly-dallying in the waiting room, then downright refusal to come with me. He would greet me at first with a smile and a good morning; then he would want to play with something in the waiting room; then to stay until he had been given his orange drink by the receptionist; then start to come upstairs and then turn back again when we had reached the first landing, then scowl at me and say he did not want to come with me. At the beginning of the week when I said that I would go upstairs and he could come up when he was ready, he came with me immediately, but later in the week his mother brought him upstairs. I could not understand this reluctance and negative behavior until it dawned on me that his mother must have said something to him about termination of treatment and that this behavior was a reaction to it. I promptly took this up with him, along the lines that he had been coming to see me because there were things that made him unhappy and that he was so much happier now, he would not need to come to see me so often, but that I would still like to see him one day each week. We would start the new arrangement after the Christmas holiday. He confirmed that this was the cause of his behavior by telling me that he did not like me and asking why he could not come to play with me every day. I replied that we were hoping that he would be going to school quite soon and then he would be playing with boys and girls, and perhaps he would not want

to come and play with me so often. He said that he would
go to school when he was a big boy like Charles—a five-year-
old who lives near his home—and that he is really a big boy
now. I agreed that he is big enough to go to school and said
that we were trying to find a nice school for him. This did
not affect the "waiting-room behavior," however, and it was
obvious that he did not want me because he felt that I did
not want him, i.e., that I did not love him if I could stop
seeing him every day. At the end of the week I interpreted
this and he hit me, saying that he didn't like me at all.

Mrs. V. reported at our interview that he had become very
clinging to her, would not let her out of his sight, and had
started waking up at nights again. She was worried about this
and wondered whether this would mean that we would continue with treatment after all. She could not remember having said anything to him about stopping treatment, as she
had understood from me that I would be taking it up with
him myself, preparing him for termination, but she had told
her husband and the grandparents of course, and she "would
not be a bit surprised if one of the grandparents had told
him, as they are so jealous of his coming here." There were
obviously overtones of her own ambivalence in this remark,
but I chose not to take it up, except to say that it is understandable that the grandparents and parents often think of a
child's therapist as a kind of rival, forgetting that the therapist
only has the child for a very short period of the day, and that
for a specific purpose. I linked up Andy's clinging behavior
with news of termination and said that we must expect the
repetition of this behavior, which would be worked through
in treatment.

WEEKLY REPORT NO. 44

Sessions 189 to 193

The "waiting-room behavior" has diminished somewhat this
week, although he still keeps me waiting for him before we

go to our room. He has also taken to showing interest in other children in the waiting room, sometimes playing with them and being loath to leave them to come with me.

During sessions he is quite forthright about his anger with me for terminating: he says that he does not like me because I do not like him. Although the transference meaning of this seems quite clear, I have not yet interpreted the transference, but have accepted his anger toward me for terminating, saying that I can understand how annoyed he must be with me. I have added, however, that he is not coming to see me every day after Christmas, *not* because I do not like him, but because he does not have the fears he used to have. I have also commented on his interest in the other children in the waiting room and he has responded by telling me their names and that they go to school.

His play has been mostly washing things in the sink. He refuses all help from me, but when I tell him he has enough water in the sink he promptly turns off the taps.

Mr. V. confirmed his wife's report of last week that Andy has become very clinging to her again. He says that she is quite anxious about treatment finishing, but he thinks she would be too shy to say anything to me about it. He tells her that I know my job and she should trust me. I spoke of such anxiety being natural, but after all I am going to see Andy once a week after Christmas and we must expect some difficulties about termination in any event—if there were *no* difficulties, I would be a bit worried myself. He thinks his wife is much better at coping with the clinging than she used to be and they both recognize that it has something to do with stopping daily treatment. Mr. V.'s new job is quite a good one. He works as a driver and finds it interesting and he is better paid than in most jobs he has had.

WEEKLY REPORT NO. 45

SESSIONS 194 TO 198

The waiting-room behavior has now almost disappeared. Early in the week I took up the transference meaning of his interpretation of the reason for termination, viz., that I did not like him. This projection was linked with his separation from his father (in his recent job, which entailed his being away from home one night a week) and from his mother (when Andy was in the hospital). I said he thought they left him because they did not like him, but it was really that *he* did not like *them* because they left him. His response to this was that he *did* like them, but he did not like me. I showed him how it is possible to like and not like the same person through his feelings about coming to see me. He was a bit tearful, saying that he would tell his mummy that I am not nice: this was interpreted as his fear that if his mummy knew (e.g., by my telling her) that sometimes he did not like her, she would think he was not nice and therefore she would stop liking him. Again I tried to show him that it is perfectly all right not to like somebody whom we like most of the time and that nothing dreadful happens at the times we don't like them.

The response to these interpretations came in my interview with Mrs. V. She reported that he has now stopped clinging to her: she can go shopping alone and at night he goes off to sleep with no difficulty. He did not wake up the previous night (the first time in the last three weeks). He has recently reverted to an old characteristic, viz., to say to her at odd moments that he loved her, but yesterday (the day of the interpretation) he surprised her by saying to her "I don't like you" when she said she was going shopping. She had said spontaneously, "That's all right, sometimes I don't like you either, but mostly I do." She was a bit surprised at herself for having said this, but she thought it must have been because of something I said to her once about everybody having mixed feelings, even toward our children. He had responded to her rejoinder by saying that she could go out to the shops by herself, *he* wasn't going to help her, but she was to bring him back a cowboy (he has a collection of plastic cowboys and Indians). When she returned he told her that he did like her after all, but sometimes she's a stinky bum and then he doesn't like her.

WEEKLY REPORT NO. 46

SESSIONS 199 TO 203   *Age 3 years and 6 months*

He has stopped the washing games which had been a feature of the last few weeks' sessions. He plays mostly with his cowboy and Indian figures which he has started bringing to the Clinic, not using any of the Clinic play material at all. The cowboys are made in such a way that parts of their bodies and equipment are interchangeable and his games are mostly concerned with taking them apart and getting me to help him reassemble them in different combinations. I am once more addressed as "friend," and on one occasion he mildly asked, "When I don't come to see you again, will it be on Monday I come to see you?" This apparently contradictory question was unraveled to mean, "When I stop coming to see you every day and come only on one day a week, will that one day be a Monday?" Nevertheless, in the way he phrased the question, he obviously recognizes that our relationship will be changed and that it is not merely a question of frequency of sessions. He is beginning to detach himself from me by bringing his own toys.

Mr. V. was unable to come to see me this week because he has recently started shift work to earn more money. He hopes to be able to come in a fortnight's time. Although I was available to speak to him on the telephone, he said he would just leave this message for me. Mrs. V. apologized to me the following day, but confirmed that the shift work was apparently unexpected. She does not like the idea very much, but it does mean more money and she will be glad of this. She is going to see a school for Andy this week.

WEEKLY REPORT NO. 47

SESSIONS 204 TO 208

Mrs. V. found the school to be not much to her liking, but at least they have offered a vacancy to Andy in January, which is more than she had had from any other school. She thinks she will try it anyway. She took Andy with her and he was fascinated to see all the boys and girls painting and he joined them straight away. He did not want to leave when it was time to go, but came away with no difficulty when she told him he would be going every day to this school after Christmas.

In his session he made no reference to school, but when I remarked that his mummy had told me about it and I asked whether he had liked it, he merely said that he had and refused to be drawn further. Another feature of his withdrawal from me occurred this week when he wanted to go to the lavatory. This wish to urinate did not seem to me to be associated, as so often in the past, with excitement. He announced that he was going to wee-wee and when I got up (I always have to switch on the light in the lavatory), he told me to stay behind, that he would go by himself. He returned shortly afterward and made no further reference to it.

His play has been mostly with trains this week, and once more he has brought the train engine from home. His train is always going on a long journey and needs lots of water and coal to make it go. The feeling that *he* may be short of water and coal when he goes away from me was interpreted, together with the transference meaning of feeling "empty" when away from his parents. He said I was silly, that when he plays trains with his daddy, the train always stops for water and coal and that his daddy says that the train won't go unless it has them. I could hardly interpret his father's con-

tinuing need for fuel from *his* parents, but contented myself
by saying that some trains might need them, but that if Andy
were a train, I was sure that he would provide his own fuel.

WEEKLY REPORT NO. 48

SESSIONS 209 TO 212

One session was missed this week, as Andy had a cold. Unlike
the pattern of the past, when this would have meant a visit to
the doctor, Mrs. V. this time decided that it was only a cold,
kept him in the house for the day, and then thought he was
well enough to come out. He had not enjoyed his day at home
and had been a great nuisance to her, agitating to get out to
play. When she told him that she was going to telephone to
me to say that he was not coming to the Clinic that day, he
had firmly told her to say that he would see me tomorrow.

For the first time he spoke spontaneously about going to
school after Christmas and when he is even bigger he will
go to the same school as his big friend, Charles. He told me,
in a comforting sort of way, that he would still come to see
me sometimes and then I could play with him and he would
show me the things Father Christmas is going to bring him.
Would Father Christmas bring me anything? What would it
be? When I asked for suggestions, he thought of new socks
and a tie, and he agreed with me when I surmised that he had
heard that his daddy was going to get these things at Christmas.
The train play continues, although the fueling does not play
such a prominent part.

WEEKLY REPORT NO. 49

SESSIONS 213 TO 217

Mrs. V. was finally able to speak of her own anxiety about
treatment finishing, primarily because Andy's sleep is once
more disturbed. She had thought that the breakdown of a
few weeks ago was the last she would hear of it, but the wak-

ing during the night has started again. I speak of this setback as temporary, as I am convinced that it is his way of expressing anxiety about termination and that we will be able to see it more clearly after the Christmas break. When he wakens he calls out and she goes into his bedroom. He insists that she leave the light on as there are tigers outside his window. When she leaves the light on he goes back to sleep quite quickly.

He made no mention of this to me, but in his play he was concerned about his train becoming lost if it should go on a long journey "without the guard" who was going to the seaside for his holiday. I interpreted this as his anxiety about himself on termination of treatment and said that he was frightened something might happen to him if he did not see me every day and that this must be like the feeling he had when he woke up during the night. He insisted that there *are* tigers outside his window, and they would eat up his belly if the light goes out, but they are frightened to come in when the light is on. I said that he was really making sure his mummy was still there and that the tigers are the pretend tigers he has inside him, i.e., his angry, biting feelings; he would like to bite me, but is afraid he will be bitten instead. His reminder to me at the end of the session to put out the light made me realize that we always need the light on during the sessions in that treatment room, and that the need for the light on at home is also an expression of his experiencing termination as a dangerous time.

WEEKLY REPORT NO. 50

SESSION 218 TO 221   *Age 3 years and 7 months*

Mrs. V. reported that the sleeping was a little improved this week. We made arrangements for the once-weekly sessions after Christmas.

He started off the week with much denial of the fact of termination. When I told him which day I would be seeing him each week after the holiday, he said, "Yes, I'll see you on Monday and Tuesday and Wednesday and Saturday and Sunday." This was followed by a swing to the other extreme: "Yes, I'll see you again when I'm a big, big boy—I'll see you when I'm eight."

He could hardly stay for the full fifty minutes each day. He was depressed, grizzly, and ready for tears at the slightest setback, e.g., when a wagon fell off his train. I said that he was very sad about not continuing to see me every day, but when he started to go to school he would not miss me so much; besides, he would be able to remember me, to think about me even when I was not there. He said he would write me letters when he learned to write at the big school—his mummy had told him he could do that. Then he said, "Friend, are you sad?" I said that I was a bit sad, because I liked seeing him every day, but I was glad too, because I knew that the only worries he had now were ones he could manage without me to help him.

On Thursday, as soon as he saw me come into the waiting room he rushed to his mother, shouting, "The card, the card" —this was a Christmas card for me and he was very proud of it. When I opened it and thanked him for it, he was very pleased indeed and told me I was to take it to my house. He kept reminding me during the session not to forget to take the card and I said he was wondering whether I would forget him and perhaps not even see him on one day a week after the holiday, but he had the answer to that one: "If you forget, my mummy will speak to you on the telephone and say that it's time you played with Andy again."

Part II

THE INDEXING OF ANDY

CHAPTER 6

GENERAL CASE MATERIAL

This part of the Index records physical and psychological aspects of the child's environment which may be of significance in their impingement on the child's development and mental functioning. It also contains relevant data about the child himself.

Sources

1. The Social History and the diagnostic interviews form the main sources of information. Any other records in the child's file should be used for additional information (e.g., interviews with parents, school reports, letters from doctors and County officials, observations made in the Clinic outside the analytic sessions, etc.).

2. Circumstances or events reported by the patient in the analytic sessions, if verified.

These data refer to the child's life before and during treatment. The child's reactions to events are recorded in this section only if observed, and as observed, in the child's environment, while reactions revealed in treatment are recorded as analytic material under the appropriate headings.

Subdivisions

This section has two subdivisions:
1. Background
2. Biographical Data

Under the heading *Background* are recorded physical and psychological data concerning the family. If the family is not the biological one (e.g., is a foster or adoptive family), appropriate information about both families should be recorded. The heading *Biographical Data* refers to details of the child's personal history, development and personality.

Background

GENERAL CASE MATERIAL: Background
CONSTELLATION OF FAMILY

Cards with this heading state, for each member of the closer family circle (father, mother, siblings) and any other persons living with the family, the name, age, and the relationship to the patient or function in the household.

Father, aged 26 at the beginning of treatment.
Mother, aged 26 at the beginning of treatment.
Andy, aged 2;5.
Paternal Grandfather and Paternal Grandmother, in whose home family have lived since marriage until recently, i.e., Andy lived with them from birth until aged 2;10. (Interview with mother and child [Chapter 3]; Weekly Report No. 16.)[1]

GENERAL CASE MATERIAL: Background
ATTITUDE TOWARD DISCIPLINE

The following four headings fall into the general group *Parents' Attitudes toward. . . .* We note here differences in attitudes between father and mother; also, if applicable, differences in attitudes toward the patient and his siblings. The heading *Attitudes toward Separations* refers to the parents' attitudes to separations of the child from his parents.

The father thinks mother tends to be too permissive toward Andy, especially in the matter of taking him into bed at night

[1] The actual text of cards is throughout indicated by condensed type. For the content of the weekly reports, see Chapter 5.

with them. On the other hand, he tolerates Andy's aggression in some areas, e.g., swearing, better than the mother does. The mother becomes impatient with him when he is disobedient, smacks him, and is then filled with remorse and apologizes to him. (Interview with mother and child [Chapter 3], Interview with parents [Chapter 4], Weekly Reports Nos. 2, 8.)

GENERAL CASE MATERIAL: Background

ATTITUDE TOWARD INSTINCTUAL MANIFESTATIONS

Mother finds difficulty in tolerating his aggression, particularly when it is expressed toward her in the form of disobedience. She was horrified at his open sexual curiosity when she found him playing with an older girl, but nevertheless Andy was able to tell her about it later, and she was able to accept the normality of this behavior when it was discussed with the therapist. (Interview with mother and child [Chapter 3], Weekly Report No. 21.)

GENERAL CASE MATERIAL: Background

ATTITUDE TOWARD SEPARATIONS

Mother is empathic about separations between mother and child; e.g., she thinks he had a bad start in life by being ill and going to the hospital. She feels that he missed frequent physical contact as a baby by being in the hospital. (Interview with mother and child [Chapter 3], Weekly Report No. 1.)

GENERAL CASE MATERIAL: Background

ATTITUDE TOWARD TREATMENT

Both parents are keen on treatment and want to do all they can to help. The mother derives much support from treatment and was able to assert herself in her maternal role during the course of it. She promptly follows any suggestion made as to amelioration of Andy's environment and in this way helps treatment considerably. Both parents use insight and information derived from the therapist to check and observe in their daily lives with Andy. (Interview with mother and child [Chapter 3], Interview with parents [Chapter 4], Weekly Report No. 2.)

GENERAL CASE MATERIAL: Background

CHARACTERISTICS OF PARENTS: Psychological

Cards under this heading contain a description of the parents' personalities, their intellectual and educational level, etc. Other headings are available for the physical characteristics of the parents, for parents' fantasies, etc.

Father: He is insightful and helpful. He has difficulty in moving away from his parents and his work history is unstable (he rarely stays in a job more than six months). (Interview with mother and child [Chapter 3], Interview with parents [Chapter 4].)

Mother: Outwardly placid, she is nevertheless frequently anxious about Andy and his behavior. She is insightful and empathic with the child to some extent, sincere and aware of her ambivalence to him. She has some hysterical symptoms, e.g., acrophobia and fear of going out in the dark unaccompanied by an adult. (Interview with mother and child [Chapter 3], Weekly Report No. 1.)

GENERAL CASE MATERIAL: Background

CHARACTERISTICS OF PARENTS: Physical

A description of the parents' appearance is desirable for all cases, especially in so far as they differ conspicuously from the average. We include deformities, invalidism, etc.

Both parents are healthy-looking young people. The mother is fairly tall, slender, with blonde hair beautifully kept. She has rather unusual green eyes. Father is very dark, with black hair and swarthy complexion. They make a strikingly handsome couple. Andy bears a marked resemblance to his mother, although his characteristic expression, unlike his mother's, is a pugnacious one. (Interview with mother and child [Chapter 3], Interview with parents [Chapter 4].)

GENERAL CASE MATERIAL: Background

ETHNIC STATUS

This heading covers information about language, nationality, religion, immigration, etc., referring to the parents. This heading also appears under the patient's *Biographical Data,* since the status of parents and patient may differ in some respects. Differences between mother and father should be noted. If any of the above is of special importance, it can be recorded on a separate card.

Family all English. (Reported by Mother, not in reports.)

GENERAL CASE MATERIAL: Background

ILLNESS IN FAMILY

Included here is information relating to any member of the family. The type of illness and length of hospitalization is to be noted. For psychological illnesses a special note should be made of any form of past or present treatment. Special headings are available for pregnancy, menopausal disturbances, abortions, accidents, addictions, deaths, etc.

Paternal grandfather is mentally disturbed (undiagnosed), his behavior suggesting hysteria, e.g., when Andy's mother had to go to the hospital with a broken arm, paternal grandfather wanted Andy to be looked after by *his* mother (almost eighty) and when Andy's mother rejected this plan, paternal grandfather had a temper tantrum, cried and threatened to commit suicide. (Interview with parents [Chapter 4].)

GENERAL CASE MATERIAL: Background

RELATIONSHIPS: Between the Parents

The heading *Relationships* refers to:
- (a) relationship between the parents
- (b) relationships of members of the family and other important persons to the patient.

This heading does not fully cover the patient's relationships with members of the family and others. See also *General Case Material: Biographical Data: Object Relationships* and Chapter 11, *Object Relationships.* Under the subheading *Relationship between the Parents* the main features of the relationship between the parents are described, e.g., harmonious and loving, frequent disagreements and quarrels, temporary separations, etc. A number of further subheadings (e.g., divorce) are provided to be used as necessary.

They are very fond of each other, and although there are difficulties arising from their individual problems, particularly sexual difficulties, they nevertheless discuss them together. They show a surprising degree of insight; e.g., the mother's sexual frigidity is seen as related to traumatic childhood experiences. The mother sees the father as being rather unreliable as far as having a steady job, but she is tolerant about this, understanding his difficulty in terms of his relationships with disturbed parents. (Interview with parents [Chapter 4], Weekly Reports Nos. 14, 27.)

(Second Indexing): During treatment, and after they had been living in their own flat for a few months, mother noticed father's increasing depression. When she asked him about it, she was shocked by his confession that he had been flirting with a young married woman, but had given her up. As the woman was associated indirectly with his job, he gave up the job and the subsequent shortage of money was given as the reason for the move back to the home of father's parents. Mother eventually accepted his behavior as being the result of his depression rather than the cause of it. (Weekly Reports Nos. 35, 38.)

GENERAL CASE MATERIAL: Background

RELATIONSHIPS: Father to Patient

He is a loving father, in some ways more tolerant of Andy's aggression than the mother is. His attitude toward Andy is less variable and apparently without the impulsive character of the mother's attitude; e.g., he uniformly takes a firmer line about such things as Andy's coming into the parental bed. (Interview with parents [Chapter 4], Weekly Reports Nos. 2, 8.)

GENERAL CASE MATERIAL: Background

RELATIONSHIPS: Mother to Patient

Basically she is a loving mother, but is in conflict over her ambivalence toward him. She is very guilty about her aggression to him and this is expressed in anxiety over even minor illnesses. She is very proud of him, but does not like this to be seen. (Interview with mother and child [Chapter 3]; Therapist's observations, not in reports.)

(Second Indexing): Late in treatment she showed herself as more accepting of her ambivalence and even verbalized it in a useful way to Andy. She was also showing signs of diminishing anxiety over his minor illnesses. (Weekly Reports Nos. 45, 48.)

GENERAL CASE MATERIAL: Background

RELATIONSHIPS: Grandparents to Patient

Generally very permissive attitude toward him. Paternal grandfather encourages Andy's acting his aggression in sadomasochistic games in which patient is allowed to hurt paternal grandfather in any way he chooses. Paternal grandfather used to say that patient is all he has to live for and if Andy goes away from paternal grandfather's home, he will commit suicide. Paternal grandmother disapproves of attempts to get patient to sleep in own bed, as she says all children go through this phase. (Interview with parents [Chapter 4], Weekly Reports Nos. 4, 5.)

GENERAL CASE MATERIAL: Background

RESIDENCE: Change of

A brief description of the type and size of the family's accommodation is given, as at the beginning of treatment. If part of the residence is sublet, any significant fact about the subtenants is recorded here. Changes of residence are noted, including those during treatment. Exceptional circumstances should be noted, e.g., the family's frequent sojourn in their country of origin.

The family removed from the home of the paternal grandparents to a flat of their own during treatment. Originally they had occupied two rooms (bed-sitting room and kitchen), later three rooms (bedroom for Andy was added). In their own flat they have three rooms and a kitchen, thus allowing for separate bedrooms for parents and Andy. These changes were due to interventions by the therapist, mainly encouragment to change, together with stressing of the importance of a separate room for Andy. (Interview with mother and child [Chapter 3], Weekly Reports Nos. 2, 4, 16.)

(Second Indexing): After a few months the family moved back to live with father's parents. This was ostensibly because their flat was too expensive, but mother ascribed it to her husband's immaturity. The move back was the result of an extramarital affair the husband had during a spell of depression. The move was grudgingly accepted by mother as she knew it would make her husband happier. (Weekly Reports Nos. 36, 37, 38.)

GENERAL CASE MATERIAL: Background

SOCIOECONOMIC STATUS

We include here statements regarding both parents' professions, occupations, sources of income (if known), social classes, and cultural and educational background. Radical changes in status should be noted.

Working class. Father earns £12 to £13 per week[2] if he works extra shifts. He changes jobs frequently. They lived in his parents' home from date of marriage until recently. Mother had tried working part-time as a shop assistant, but this lasted only a few weeks because of difficulties with Andy. (Interview with mother and child [Chapter 3], Interview with parents [Chapter 4].)

Biographical Data

GENERAL CASE MATERIAL: Biographical Data

DEVELOPMENTAL DATA AND MILESTONES: Birth

Delivery was normal and took place in the hospital. He was 7 lbs. at birth. (Interview with mother and child [Chapter 3].)

---

[2] About $35 per week, equivalent perhaps to an income of $70 per week in urban United States.

GENERAL CASE MATERIAL: Biographical Data

DEVELOPMENTAL DATA AND MILESTONES: Feeding

He was breast-fed for the first three weeks of life, but after the first ten days he started to lose weight and had diarrhea. Following admission to the hospital with gastroenteritis at three weeks he was bottle-fed. He continued to be bottle-fed until the age of two years, since he developed diarrhea whenever solids were introduced into his diet. When he did start on solids, there was no further difficulty, and he had no food fads at the time of referral. (Interview with mother and child [Chapter 3], Weekly Report No. 28.)

GENERAL CASE MATERIAL: Biographical Data

DEVELOPMENTAL DATA AND MILESTONES: Habit Training

This was started when he was seven months old and he was dry and clean between sixteen and eighteen months old. Although he has remained clean since then, he started to wet his trousers slightly at the age of two years three months and this was the position at the start of treatment. (Interview with mother and child [Chapter 3].)

GENERAL CASE MATERIAL: Biographical Data

DEVELOPMENTAL DATA AND MILESTONES: Talking

He had three or four words at the age of eighteen months (Interview with mother and child [Chapter 3].)

GENERAL CASE MATERIAL: Biographical Data

DEVELOPMENTAL DATA AND MILESTONES: Walking

He started to walk at about the age of one year. (Interview with mother and child [Chapter 3].)

GENERAL CASE MATERIAL: Biographical Data

DEVELOPMENTAL DATA AND MILESTONES: Weaning

Weaning took place when he was admitted to the hospital at the age of three weeks and he was then bottle-fed. Weaning from the bottle took place at two years. (Interview with mother and child [Chapter 3], Weekly Report No. 28.)

GENERAL CASE MATERIAL: Biographical Data

ETHNIC STATUS

English by nationality and in language. (Reported by mother, not in reports.)

GENERAL CASE MATERIAL: Biographical Data

EVENT WITH POSSIBLE TRAUMATIC EFFECT

Therapists record here, either at the first or subsequent indexings, any events or series of events which they consider to have been of traumatic significance for the child.

Difficulty and pain on micturition led to the discovery of adhesion of foreskin to glans penis, at the age of twenty-two months. Circumcision was at first recommended, but was found to be unnecessary. The adhesions were broken by stretching of the foreskin; this was done at an outpatient clinic, the child being forcibly held down by two attendants and it occasioned pain. Andy has made various references to putting a pin in somebody's winkie or having one put in his. (Weekly Reports Nos. 4, 11.)

GENERAL CASE MATERIAL: Biographical Data

HOSPITALIZATION

For each of patient's hospitalizations, age, reason for duration and frequency of the parents' visits should be noted, as well as the patient's reactions during hospitalization and after return.

Although he was aged only two years five months at referral he had already been hospitalized three times:
1. At the age of three weeks until four months for gastroenteritis. Although his mother visited daily, there was little physical contact with him, because she usually had to see him through a glass partition. She was occasionally allowed to feed him.

2. At the age of eight months for two days with bronchitis. His mother was in the hospital at the same time with a broken arm —and she was unable to visit him.

3. At the age of eighteen months for twenty-four hours for observation following a febrile convulsion. He was visited by mother. (Interview with mother and child [Chapter 3], Weekly Report No. 28.)

GENERAL CASE MATERIAL: Biographical Data

ILLNESS AND MEDICAL TREATMENT: Physical

A separate heading is also available for psychological illness.

1. Gastroenteritis, aet. three weeks to four months; treated in hospital.
2. Convulsions, aet. one yr. and eighteen months.
3. Adhesion of foreskin to glans penis, treated by stretching.
4. Frequent colds and bronchitis; on one occasion he was treated in the hospital for two days, general treatment and occasionally treated by penicillin (orally and intramuscularly in buttocks). (Interview with mother and child [Chapter 3], Weekly Report No. 11.)

GENERAL CASE MATERIAL: Biographical Data

OBJECT RELATIONSHIPS

This heading refers to relationships (past and present) of the *patient* to members of his family (including previous members of the household) and others; and also to the use of transitional objects. Features of the child's object relationships should be noted here.

The heading serves especially for the recording of data from external sources, which did not emerge in the treatment. If such data do appear in the treatment material, they are recorded with the relevant analytic material in the section *Object Relationships*.

At the diagnostic interview there were obvious signs of a close relationship with the mother, in which he did not verbalize his needs, but she seemed to understand them and fulfill them. He seemed able to tolerate a certain amount of frustration from her, albeit with a struggle. Relationships with other children were aggressive, with the exception of one quiet and gentle boy with whom Andy was friendly and nonaggressive. (Interview with mother and child [Chapter 3].)

GENERAL CASE MATERIAL: Biographical Data

OBJECT RELATIONSHIPS: Inanimate Objects

His mother reported that as a baby he used to take a blue cuddly dog to bed with him, but gave it up at the age of one and a half years. (Mother's statement, not in reports.)

GENERAL CASE MATERIAL: Biographical Data

PERSONALITY TRAITS: Aggressive

Cards are made under this heading for every patient, and a separate card is prepared for every significant character trait. The material entered is descriptive and includes information gathered from external sources as well as the therapist's observations. The analytic findings will be listed under the appropriate headings in other sections. Changes in character traits observed during treatment should be noted.

He was thought of as a very aggressive child, especially toward other children. (Interview with mother and child [Chapter 3].)

GENERAL CASE MATERIAL: Biographical Data

PERSONALITY TRAITS: Restless

He was described as restless, to a degree that made the mother feel that he was wearing himself out. (Interview with mother and child [Chapter 3].)

GENERAL CASE MATERIAL: Biographical Data

PHYSICAL AND MEDICAL CHARACTERISTICS: Patient's Appearance

Cards under this heading contain a description of the patient's appearance at the beginning of treatment. Changes during treatment are noted.

He was a sturdy little boy with blond hair and red cheeks, and greenish eyes. His expression varied between pugnacity and impishness. Most people find him attractive, to judge by the frequent remarks to that effect by people in the waiting room and by staff members. (Interview with mother and child [Chapter 3], Therapist's observations.)

GENERAL CASE MATERIAL: Biographical Data

SCHOOL: Starting Age

(Second Indexing): He started nursery school immediately on changing from intensive treatment to once-weekly sessions, at the age of three years seven months, and settled extremely well at school.

GENERAL CASE MATERIAL: Biographical Data

SEPARATIONS: From Father

Separations are noted, whether caused through the absence of the patient from home or through the absence of the parents. An indication should be given of the persons caring for the child during the separation, and the reactions of the patient to the separation, if reported.

Separations were occasioned by Andy's going to the hospital and were, therefore, from both parents. (Interview with mother and child [Chapter 3].)

GENERAL CASE MATERIAL: Biographical Data

SEPARATIONS: From Mother

Separations were occasioned by Andy's going to the hospital. (Interview with mother and child [Chapter 3].)

CHAPTER 7

EGO: GENERAL

Ego: General

CONTROL OF DRIVE ACTIVITY

These cards should include illustrations of strength or weakness of the functions controlling drive activity, as in impulsive behavior, inability to tolerate frustration or to postpone gratification, acting out, irruption of primary process into secondary process thinking, etc. Where control depends on either the presence of, support from, or reassurance by an external object, the appropriate subheading should be used.

This was inadequate, especially of aggressive drives, e.g., when angered he would throw things and attack the therapist. Later in treatment there were signs of strengthening control; e.g., sometimes when throwing things about he obviously took care that the therapist was not hit; again, one day when Andy was angry with the therapist, instead of kicking him as he would have done earlier, he contented himself with making kicking motions in the air. When the therapist remarked that Andy knew the therapist did not like having heavy things thrown at him, Andy was able to stop doing so, but translated the aggression into words, saying that he did not like the therapist and addressed him as "stinky bum." (Weekly Reports Nos. 12, 15, 19, 21, 22.)

(Second Indexing): Control of aggressive drives became more and more adequate as treatment progressed. Throwing things at the therapist, and other active attacks, diminished until they disap-

peared, to be replaced by verbalization. (Weekly Reports Nos. 44, 45.)

Ego: General

IDENTIFICATION

The term identification covers certain usages of the terms introjection and incorporation in the literature. It is defined here as the appropriation by the individual of a mental or physical attribute, real or fantasied, of the object world, becoming or being treated as part of the self or the ideal self, permanently or temporarily. Although identification is a process serving ego development in general, it can be put to specific defensive use. This happens when such appropriations from the external world are made to avoid or mitigate external or internal threats or dangers. If this is the case, the text cards should be placed under the appropriate *Defense* heading.

Included in this section will be cards illustrating certain ego responses to superego figures, e.g., the child feeling like, behaving like, or professing the standards of admired, respected, or feared objects or their internal representatives. In view of the fact that processes of identification take place both in ego and superego development, a further research is in progress to attempt to clarify the criteria for classification. For the time being all text cards emphasizing identification should be placed here. It should be noted whether the identification is transient or enduring and the role of active and conscious imitation should be mentioned where appropriate.

Separate subheadings are available for "as if" types of identification, counter and negative identifications, temporary "merging" with another person, etc.

Early in treatment there was a certain amount of fluidity in his identification; i.e., his behavior showed identification with the mother as a housewife, mother or wife; and with father as husband, worker, and father; and these would alternate from day to day. Later, however, his principal identification was with the father as somebody active who goes out driving big lorries. When this identification first appeared, it was a confused picture of the father which he presented, inasmuch as the father was active in his lorry driving but was motherly and protective at the same time. Later it was the active aspect of the identification which predominated by far. (Weekly Reports Nos. 7, 8, 9, 12, 24, 27, 28.)

Ego: General

INTEGRATION: Emergence of

Cards placed under this heading should include examples of the beginnings of integration in any area of ego functioning. By integration in this context is meant a tendency inherent in the ego to unify all the elements at its disposal. Cards should cover

(a) the process of integrating;

(b) the nature of the elements integrated, a distinction being made between integration of sensory data (pleasure-pain expectation, the recognition of sources of pleasure and pain, etc.), and integration within structures. A child may have a well-integrated ego, but with part of the ego left out of the synthesis;

(c) the result of integration;

(d) the ability to integrate. Defective functioning should be indexed here.

Material referring to a deficiency in or lack of integration, as well as to processes of disintegration, are recorded under alternative headings.

This was indicated in his mother's report of an improvement in the sleep disturbance. At a particular stage of the treatment she reported that although he still awoke during the night, he did not need to see her—she had only to call out to him that she was there and he went back to sleep immediately. This was understood as his having become able to connect sensory data and memories and use them in a process of logical thinking to control anxiety. (Weekly Report No. 5.)

Ego: General

INTEGRATION

(Second Indexing): During the latter stages of treatment, evidence of an established integrative process was seen in his use of an interpretation. This interpretation related to ambivalence, and was made in several stages:

1. It was evident that he thought termination was being brought about because the therapist did not like him. This projection was linked with separations from the original objects and he was told that the real situation was that he did not like them (and the therapist) because they left him. His response to this was to say that he *did* like them, but *not* the therapist.

2. He was shown, through his feelings about the therapist, that it is possible to like and not like the same person. His response to this was tearfulness and a threat to tell his mummy that the therapist was not nice.

3. This further projection was interpreted as his fear that if his mummy knew that sometimes he did not like her, she would think him not nice. The therapist made the statement that it is perfectly all right not to like somebody whom we like most of the time and that nothing dreadful happens at the times we do not like them.

On the following day, when his mother told him she was going shopping, he told her he did not like her. When she responded that sometimes she did not like him, but mostly she *did* like him, he replied that she could go by herself. This seems to have been taken by him as a confirmation of the interpretation and the event was concomitant with a cessation of clinging behavior and a recent sleep disturbance. This is understood as integration of thought processes, following on remembering the interpretation, testing it out and assessing its efficacy. The process led to a behavioral change, following on active mastery of anxiety. (Weekly Report No. 45.)

Ego: General

INTELLIGENCE

A card recording the intelligence test results is made out for every patient. Cards should, in addition to stating the I.Q. and the test or tests applied, state agreement or discrepancy between mental age and performance. Deficiency in abstract thinking is indexed elsewhere.

No formal testing was undertaken at the beginning of treatment, but the therapist estimates child's intelligence to be within the range "above average—superior." (Therapist's observations, not recorded in reports.)

(Second Indexing): Testing was done on termination of intensive treatment. Results were I.Q. 118 on Revised Stanford-Binet, Form "L." The mother, who was present during the testing, thought that Andy did as well as he was able to, but the psychologist wondered whether lack of familiarity with nursery type of material did not affect his results. Andy showed very good verbal ability.

EGO: General

LANGUAGE: Speech

This subheading covers the function of speech and its developmental aspect. Manifestations of disturbance, e.g., retardation of speech development, echolalia, parroting, etc., should be placed here. Other headings are provided for the use of language (e.g., bizarre) and verbalization, while the *Symptoms* section provides headings for disturbances of speech.

This is well developed in content and he uses many words and phrases not usually associated with children of his age. He uses these appropriately and this seems to derive from the active encouragement of the grandparents to use "grown-up words." As part of this accomplishment he has a large stock of swearwords, and these too he uses freely, either aggressively or seductively or in sheer enjoyment. His mother objects to his using swearwords and scolds him for it, with the result that he used them provocatively. Soon after the start of treatment she reported that he swore only at the Clinic and not outside it. (Weekly Reports Nos. 2, 3, 9, 12, 16.)

(Second Indexing): Toward the end of treatment, swearing was discontinued in sessions as well as outside them. (Therapist's observations, not in reports.)

Ego: General

LANGUAGE: Verbalization, Use of

Cards placed under this heading should refer to the good or poor ability to verbalize. They should give illustrations of the use of substitutes for and earlier modes of expression of verbalization (e.g., acting out, blushing, wriggling, motor behavior, silences, and "body language" in general).

Andy has a good capacity for verbalization of his wishes, needs, likes and dislikes, although verbalization is often accompanied by action. He expresses fantasies freely in words and early in treatment told the therapist simple stories built around his fantasies.

As substitutes for verbalization, as distinguished from actions accompanying verbalization, he sometimes uses some form of direct physical contact, e.g., pinching or stroking. Other substitutes are the impulsive throwing of articles and rushing around the room.

Verbalization of affect is well developed for a child of his age; e.g., he will say he is annoyed or angry and on one occasion he said he was sad. (Weekly Reports Nos. 8, 9, 12, 16, 18, 20, 28.)

Ego: General

MOTILITY

All aspects of the child's motility may be indexed here if significant. Motor disturbances may also be found under *Symptoms.*

Ordinarily he is very motile, but in control of his body at such times; e.g., he will spend several minutes on a circular tour of the furniture in the treatment room, climbing from chair to table, jumping from table to couch, then from couch to a smaller table and so on. He will do this rapidly and never once has he fallen. On the other hand, he sometimes rushes around the room apparently aimlessly and in great excitement and at such times he is liable to slip and he has banged his head once or twice during such activities, probably because the aggression was being turned against the self. (Weekly Reports Nos. 4, 5, 12, 16.)

(Second Indexing): His restlessness was later seen to be also anxiety-driven and to subserve the function of discharging tension; e.g., during a time of marital upset between his parents he was extremely restless, dashing about the room and changing activities very frequently. (Weekly Report No. 36.)

EGO: General

PLAY

Cards placed here should record what is typical for the child or unusual for his age or sex; the absence of play; stereotyped play; the incapacity for imaginative or fantasy play; and lack of pleasure in play.

At the beginning of treatment Andy's play was imaginative and involved the use of a variety of inanimate objects such as toy animals and dolls. The fantasies associated with his play contained such large aggressive and sadomasochistic elements, however, that it soon degenerated into wild throwing, sometimes at the therapist.

With interpretation of the fantasies, play gradually assumed a more constructive character; the imaginativeness was retained and play more and more involved the therapist as a playmate as well as a transference object. This change was reflected in his reported increased ability to play happily with other children instead of his former aggressiveness. (Interview with mother and child [Chapter 3], Weekly Reports Nos. 1, 2, 3, 4, 8, 12, 14, 22, 24.)

EGO: General

REALITY, RELATION TO EXTERNAL

Material indexed under this heading should show adaptation or nonadaptation to external reality; the prevalent manner of adaptation, i.e., whether autoplastic or alloplastic.

This is soundly established. Andy is well aware of external reality and its dangers and takes appropriate, but not excessive, steps to avoid such dangers; e.g., he pretended to be about to fall downstairs but made sure the therapist was near enough to catch him; on another occasion he said he was going to fall off the couch, but when no steps were taken to protect him, he put a cushion on the floor and fell on that. (Weekly Reports Nos. 4, 5.)

Ego: General

REALITY, RELATION TO EXTERNAL: Reality Testing

This is one of the subheadings under the previous heading. It refers to the ability to recognize external reality and its dangers and to differentiate fantasy from reality. Both general and temporary disturbances in this capacity should be recorded. Disturbances in the cathexis of external reality are recorded under a separate subheading.

Differentiation between fantasy and external reality is mostly sound, although occasionally it fails; e.g., on hearing thunder one day he was sure it was a tiger in the sky; on another occasion he insisted that a doll had a winkie when it patently had not. (Weekly Report No. 7; Therapist's observation, not in reports.)

Ego: General

SUMMARY: Stability of Ego

This indicates the degree to which the ego functions of secondary autonomy remain stable in the face of threats, external or internal. Cards belong here which show the ease or difficulty for the child to regress to former stages of ego development or to lower forms of functioning, or the frequency with which such regressions occur.

His ego is adequately stable for his stage of development. There is a tendency to regress when under threat (internal) of displacement by a rival or of being left by the mother. In treatment, this tendency is quantitatively slight and transitory, and takes the forms of crawling up and downstairs, asking to be carried, and "baby talk"; on one occasion he wet his trousers at the end of a session. (Weekly Reports Nos. 2, 5, 7, 9, 16.)

CHAPTER 8

EGO: ANXIETY

For the purpose of indexing material here anxiety is understood as an affect experienced by the ego when it perceives or anticipates a danger situation which contains a threat to the maintenance of psychic equilibrium. This threat can come from the external world, the id, or the superego. The ego's reactions will differ according to whether it is (1) temporarily overwhelmed by an unmanageable quantity of excitation or (2) whether a small, manageable amount of anxiety is experienced in its function as a danger signal. The main groups of headings in the section include cards referring to the contents arousing anxiety, and to the types of ego response to anxiety.

EGO: ANXIETY: Contents Arousing Anxiety

THREATS TO INTEGRITY OF BODY: Castration

In the various subsections of *Contents Arousing Anxiety* the aim is not to record all the contents that are observed to arouse anxiety in the child, but rather to note those which are apt to arouse particularly large amounts of anxiety or which do so either frequently or always, or which are in some other way of special note. The cards should specify as far as possible the instinctual impulse, affect, fantasy, activity, external situation or object that, typically for the child (or for certain developmental phases, e.g., adolescence), evoke anxiety. They should also indicate the mode of expression of the anxiety, and give illustrative examples. If the anxiety is shown in the form of a specific fear or dread, both the manifest fear and its unconscious determinants should be indicated. Care should be taken to trace and record, as far as possible, the underlying conflict in its structural and dynamic aspects. For the subheading the deepest layer understood and interpreted should be chosen.

The subheading *Threats to Integrity of Body* is part of a group which contains such threats as castration, starvation, change of body, attacks, physical punishment, etc.

Threats to the integrity of the self (e.g., annihilation, disintegration, loss of identity, loss of control, etc.), including anxieties about persecution, are placed under another group of subheadings.

Castration was feared, expressed often as fear of being bitten. This was seen mainly in fantasies, but provoked the actual covering up of the penis with his hand or the need to urinate (seen as an anxiety-driven need for reassurance as to the continuing integrity of his penis); e.g., immediately after telling the therapist the simple story "somebody put a pin in a little boy's winkie," he rushed to the door saying he wanted a wee-wee. He did not wait for help from his mother as he usually did at that time, but went straight to the lavatory and urinated. (Weekly Reports Nos. 4, 10, 11.)

EGO: ANXIETY: Contents Arousing Anxiety

SITUATIONS AND OBJECTS: Being Left by the Mother

In the headings under *Situations and Objects* the emphasis is, apart from the description of the manifest reaction, on the following aspects:

1. Historical: A specific situation, real or felt to be real, may represent an earlier one (e.g., being left alone by the mother may represent a repetition of an earlier traumatic separation experience).

2. Instinctual: Anxiety is aroused by sexual or aggressive impulses, the internal danger being displaced onto an external situation. For example, due to hostile or libidinal wishes the separation from the love object may mean danger either to the self (via retaliation) or to the object.

3. Object relationship: This aspect of the anxiety is related to the specific role which the (external or internal) object has for the child. For example, separation from the need-satisfying object may mean starvation or helplessness; separation may be experienced as loss of an auxiliary ego; or anxiety may be aroused by externalized superego figures.

This is based historically on his various hospitalizations. At frequent intervals during the treatment he will not come to the treatment room without his mother, although most often he can allow her to leave after a few minutes. He usually expresses the anxiety in crying, screaming or saying he wants his mummy with him and often asks her where she is going when she leaves the room, although he knows she spends the time in the waiting room and is always there at the end of his session. (Interview with mother and child [Chapter 3], Weekly Report No. 3.)

(Second Indexing): Dynamically, anxiety in this situation was more clearly evaluated in relation to termination of treatment, i.e., in the transference. Being left by the mother (therapist) aroused his aggression and hatred; the aggression and hatred were then projected onto the object and he experienced anxiety, feeling that love was being aggressively withdrawn. Following interpretations this anxiety ceased. (Weekly Reports Nos. 43, 44, 45.)

EGO: ANXIETY: Types of Ego Response

SIGNAL ANXIETY LEADING TO EGO ACTIVITY: Use of Persons

The *Types of Ego Response* refer to both the ego's coping with the anxiety that is felt and with the danger it indicates. The subheadings attempt to differentiate between (1) the ego that is flooded and overwhelmed with anxiety upon the perception of a danger (threat), and (2) the ego that experiences anxiety as a danger signal and reacts actively to cope with the danger it signifies. Cards may cover immediate or delayed reactions, and should illustrate both habitual and specific modes of coping. A broad distinction is made between anxiety attacks or states of panic on the one hand, and signal anxiety leading to ego activity on the other. This latter subsection contains permanent cross-references to such headings as *Ego (Defenses); Fantasies; Symptoms;* and *Superego (Ego Response).*

Under the specific heading *Use of Persons* are classified instances in which the child uses external persons as "auxiliary egos" to help his weak ego to cope with the anxiety or threat. Also included here are appeals to higher powers in the form of prayers, magical acts, etc.

He used persons, particularly his mother, to reinforce his ego; e.g., when he awoke at night, he would call out for his mother. When she responded by calling out to him, he was able to go back to sleep again. (Weekly Report No. 5.)

CHAPTER 9

EGO: DEFENSES

The term "defense" is used here as a general term to designate mechanisms and functions which the psychic apparatus can employ to keep away from consciousness unpleasurable psychic contents and instinctual wishes or their derivatives that are not ego syntonic. Certain defense mechanisms have been defined, being specific methods used by the ego for such purposes. They work automatically and outside consciousness.

The list of subheadings in this section has been divided into three groups:

1. General Characteristics
2. Defense Mechanisms
3. Other Defensive Measures

A distinction between defense mechanisms and defensive measures was found necessary, since it is not always possible to pick out the specific defense mechanism or combination of mechanisms in a manifestation which clearly is of defensive character or which serves defensive purposes. Instead, it is possible that all ego functions and activities may be utilized for the purposes of defense. The subsection *Defensive Measures* makes it possible to record such complex defensive manifestations. If, at some later time, the mechanism or mechanisms involved should become clear, this is noted under the original

heading and cross-references to the relevant *Mechanism* headings are made.

Cards indexed under specific defense headings should contain the following points:

1. The type of defense, or the defensive measure used.

2. A note of whether the defense was used in relation to
particular anxieties, or whether it was used more generally.

3. The specific anxiety-producing content which is defended against.

4. An example of the operation of the defense.

5. A quantitative assessment (e.g., excessive, occasional),
where relevant.

6. An indication of whether the defense was prevalent in a
particular phase of treatment (or throughout treatment).

If the child uses a combination of defenses which is specific
for him, careful cross-referencing to the individual defenses is
indicated. The text is indexed first under the most prominent
defense, and the other defenses involved are stated in paren-
theses. There are a number of permanent cross-references
(guide cards) linking various related defenses, e.g., *Passive
into Active* has a guide card to *Reversal of Roles, Identification with the Aggressor, Domineering,* and *Denial in Fantasy.*

EGO: DEFENSES: General Characteristics

Cards which are placed in this section should refer to features
of defense which are recurrent or general in the case. They
should provide a descriptive summary, and dynamic, structural, genetic, and quantitative aspects should be included
in the text. Special subheadings refer to the excessive use
of defenses, to the multiplicity of defenses, the paucity of
defenses, and the untimely use of defenses.

Defenses are mainly of a primitive type, with displacement and
denial in fantasy as those most generally used, although projection and regression were also common. All defenses were labile
and easily broke down, particularly defenses against aggressive

impulses toward loved objects. With the breakdown of the defenses, anxiety was more evident.

(Second Indexing): During the latter part of treatment, some rearrangement of the defensive structure could be seen; displacement was much less used and there was no evidence of denial in fantasy at all. Projection and regression were still used, although they were soon replaced by turning passive into active; this last defense was the one eventually used to cope with termination, and it was maintained ego-syntonically at least up to the time of indexing.

EGO: DEFENSES: Defense Mechanisms

DISPLACEMENT

Displacement as a defense mechanism occurs when an id impulse or an affect is felt or expressed toward a substitute object (person, animal, or thing) because its expression toward the original object would arouse anxiety.

This was the most frequently used mechanism, although as regards his aggressive impulses it was used in rapid alternation with direct expression of aggression against the object; e.g., in the same session he would attack the wash basin or towel rail for a time, then attack the therapist, switching back again to the substitute object and so on.

Displacement was also much used in expressing fear—dogs, cats, thunder, being displacement of fear from the father; e.g., at a stage when his castration anxiety was acute, his mother reported that he would not go near any dog or cat in the street as he said they might bite him. Gee-gees, wolves, and monkeys were prominent in this mechanism as substitute objects for father. (Weekly Reports Nos. 4, 5, 9, 10, 11, 12, 15; Mother's statement, not in reports.)

(Second Indexing): In the later stages of treatment there were economic shifts in the use of this defense; viz., it was less used in dealing with his aggressive impulses, and also the rapid alternation between displacement and direct expression of aggression disappeared to all intents and purposes. (Weekly Reports Nos. 42, 44, 45.)

EGO: DEFENSES: Defense Mechanisms

IDENTIFICATION WITH THE AGGRESSOR (AND DISPLACEMENT)

Identification with the aggressor implies the warding off of an anticipated attack by identifying with the threatening aspect of the feared person and actively turning aggression against this person or others.

This defense was commonly used in conjunction with displacement; e.g., his aggression would be displaced onto an animal, say a cat, and he warned the therapist that pussies always bite. At that time he was afraid of cats. He then identified with the pussy, miaowing and eventually scratching. At this time he had been the victim of his cousin George who bit him on the abdomen and drew blood. (Weekly Reports Nos. 22, 23.)

EGO: DEFENSES: Defense Mechanisms

PASSIVE INTO ACTIVE

This is a repeating actively of a passively endured past experience, real or felt to be real. This defense is also an element in several other defenses.

Much of his aggressive play was based on this defense, the aggression which he felt as being directed against him coming mainly from his fantasies; e.g., when he spoke of various animals (gee-gee, wolves, monkeys, etc.) as going to hit him, bite him and so on, he would speak of his intention to attack them, and in fact attack them in effigy in the form of dolls, toy animals, plasticine.

However, when faced with real aggression, he also used this mechanism; e.g., one day when a little girl hit him on the head with a stick, he promptly went out into the street and hit a little boy. (Weekly Reports Nos. 3, 13.)

(Second Indexing): This defense was the principal one used to cope with termination—instead of being left, he gradually left the treatment situation. At first he indicated this by bringing toys from home to play with during sessions instead of the well-loved ones kept at the Clinic, and finally during the latter stages of the nonintensive part of treatment he was almost completely uninterested in the interviews. (Weekly Report Nos. 46, 47.)

EGO: DEFENSES: Defense Mechanisms

PASSIVE INTO ACTIVE: Anticipation by Provocation

Cards indexed here refer to one particular form of *Passive into Active*. It consists of the warding off of a painful past experience, passively endured, the repetition of which is expected and feared, by taking the active part in bringing it about through provocation (e.g., the child may provoke rejection by difficult or aggressive behavior in order to forestall the repetition of a past passive experience of having been deserted).

Another subheading deals with the particular form of *Passive into Active* which has been called *Anticipation by Action*. It is the doing to oneself, in fact or in fantasy, of something unpleasant that the child expects to be done to him by another person in the future. This is a defense against passive surrender by taking over the role of attacker toward oneself (e.g., the child who plays at taking out his own tonsils before an operation).

He fears being left by the mother, sometimes even by withdrawal of attention, and defends against this by drawing attention to himself by provocative behavior. The withdrawal he sees as aggression directed toward him; so he actively provokes aggression to avoid being the passive party. In treatment on an occasion when he was furious with the therapist he threw a doll which hit a tumbler with a ringing noise. He exclaimed: "My goodness, you frightened me out of your life." When this was interpreted as his own anger frightening him, but that it would not frighten the therapist, who would not leave him even if he *is* angry, Andy came very close to the therapist and shouted "Fuckie, fuckie" into his face in a very provocative manner. This was understood as a provocation of rejection. (Weekly Reports Nos. 3, 6.)

(Second Indexing): There was a marked shift away from this procedure later in treatment. Although the mother reported a lessening of provocative behavior at home, this shift is best exemplified by his way of dealing with the impending termination of treatment, which he at first took to be his being left by the therapist

(mother). At one time this would have produced behavior which would have been intended to provoke rejection, but in fact he dealt with the threatening situation eventually by an increasing withdrawal of cathexis from the therapist (seen at first in his bringing toys from home to sessions instead of using the Clinic toys), i.e., he was turning passive into active, but not through anticipation by provocation. (Weekly Reports Nos. 46, 47.)

Ego: Defenses: Defense Mechanisms

PROJECTION

The term "projection" as used in its defensive sense here refers to the warding off of an idea, affect, or drive derivative by ascribing it to the external world. Conscious cathexis is not necessarily withdrawn from the unwanted internal content, but the content is displaced onto another person where it impresses the child as a threat or danger, aggressive or seductive, coming from the external world.

Instances may also be included here in which only the first step of this process can be clearly discerned (externalization of internal content). Cards should state clearly what is projected, e.g., aggression, guilt feelings, etc.

This mechanism was seen sometimes as only externalization of drive derivatives without these then being felt to be a threat to him from the external world, e.g., he frequently asserted that other people stink or are naughty. It was also seen in full flower, however, where the externalized content was then experienced as a threat; e.g., one day when he was angry with the therapist, he fell to the floor and said: "*You* did that." It was seen also in his many fantasies of being bitten or attacked by various animals, and this was understood as a projection of his aggression. (Weekly Reports Nos. 9, 21.)

Ego: Defenses: Defense Mechanisms

REGRESSION

Cards under this heading should show the specific anxiety or danger defended against, the developmental levels from which and to which regression takes place, whether the regression affects the drives, ego development, or object relationships, and whether it is temporary or of a more permanent character.

The danger defended against was of being left or replaced and the mechanism came into play in relation to the mother, both in reality and in the transference. It was seen as a temporary phenomenon, not a deep regression, yet fairly easily and frequently used at one stage in the treatment. It usually took the form of regression to the oral dependent level, when he would ask to be picked up and carried or he would crawl upstairs. He could verbalize his wish to regress, and in the verbalization was contained the clue to the anxiety defended against; e.g., he would often ask his mother to confirm that he *is* her little darling, he *is* her little baby. (Weekly Reports Nos. 2, 5, 6, 7.)

(Second Indexing): In the terminal stages of treatment, there was an interesting use of this defense. When faced with the danger of being left, regressive behavior with the real mother appeared (clinging, sleep disturbance), but not with the mother in the transference. The regression fluctuated over the last few weeks of treatment, finally showing signs of disappearing again. (Weekly Reports Nos. 43, 44, 45, 49, 50.)

Ego: Defenses: Defense Mechanisms

REVERSAL OF ROLES

This type of *Reversal* applies to the case where the child takes over the role of an adult or a more powerful child and simultaneously makes the other person into the child.

This was a prominent defense in a recent phase of treatment. It appeared in his assertion that he was the daddy and the therapist the baby. As this was a time when he was displaying some anxiety about his father's absence from home one evening each week, it was first interpreted as his wish to be able to tell the therapist what to do. He thereupon caressed the therapist and called him his little daddy. The following day the therapist was made even smaller by being made into a little girl in which role Andy as the daddy took him shopping and then to a clinic. (Weekly Report No. 23.)

Ego: Defenses: Defense Mechanisms

REVERSAL OF AFFECT: Prestage

Reversal is regarded as the warding off of a dangerous drive derivative by substituting its opposite (e.g., an active drive is turned into its passive counterpart, or vice versa). This can, but need not, lead to a permanent change within the personality, secured by permanent anticathexes (i.e., becoming reaction formations).

The subheading *Reversal of Affect* refers to a change in the quality of the experienced affect. Cards must show the opposite affect displayed. This heading is to be distinguished from *Denial, Repression, Isolation* (of affect from content), *Displacement* (onto other objects), etc.

Prestages of the mechanism of *Reversal of Affect* may also be described here; e.g., denigrating the love object; attempting to make the loved object into a hateful one (by magic or otherwise), etc.

Denigration of the love object was often seen in the transference, where he would call the therapist abusive, anal names, although the affect was sometimes a loving one. That this was a prestage of reversal was seen in the ease with which the affect would then be changed to antagonism and anger; e.g., following an interpretation of his wish to do with the therapist what daddy does with mummy, he lovingly called the therapist a "fuckie-bogie" and smiled, but this was then followed by an aggressive outburst directed at the therapist. (Weekly Report No. 12.)

(Second Indexing): During the rest of the treatment there was no indication that he had gone beyond the prestage of this defense to full-blown reversal of affect. In fact, his affects have remained readily available to him in undisguised form, e.g., anger, indignation, pleasure, regret, depression, and sadness. (Weekly Reports Nos. 29, 37, 38, 50.)

EGO: DEFENSES: Defense Mechanisms

TURNING AGAINST THE SELF OF AGGRESSION (AND PROJECTION)

In material indexed under this heading, instances should be given where an id impulse, usually of an aggressive kind, is withdrawn from the object toward which it is directed in the external world and employed instead against the self. Cards should indicate the object toward whom the aggressive impulse was directed. An attempt should also be made to distinguish between defense

(a) against the aggressive impulse (where it is transferred from its object to the self);

(b) against guilt feelings for an aggressive act committed, in fact or in fantasy, shown by injuring the self afterwards (self-punishment);

(c) the provocation of injury by others as a defense against either aggressive trends or guilt for aggressive actions.

This defense was not often used and then commonly in association with projection. It was seen in two forms, viz., as a defense against an aggressive impulse and as self-punishment for an aggressive act. At one session, after he told a story of a gee-gee who bit a boy, and after his dislike of being bitten was verbalized by the therapist, he bit the toy gee-gee and threw it away. His wish to bite was then interpreted as giving rise to his fear of being bitten and he threw the toys about the room. At the end of the session he ran straight into the wall, bumping his head, and he started to cry. This was interpreted as his having hurt himself because he was afraid of hurting somebody else. On another occasion he had kicked the therapist's head at the end of a session. His first action the following day was to fall back against the couch and slide to the floor, saying that the little pussy had hurt himself. This was seen as self-punishment. (Weekly Reports Nos. 3, 9, 12.)

(Second Indexing): No further examples of this mechanism were seen during the rest of the treatment.

EGO: DEFENSES: Other Defensive Measures

DENIAL IN WORD AND ACTION

Denial is regarded as the refusal to acknowledge unpleasant reality, external or internal. Denial is distinguished from repression in that what is predominant is a withdrawal of attention cathexis from the unpleasant reality, while in repression this is reinforced by anticathexes.

Denial in Word and Action represents a normal "prestage of defense" at an early developmental level, but it is of highly pathological significance in later phases when the ego functions of perception, memory, and reality testing normally counteract it.

His delaying behavior in coming to sessions, although often provocative, was also seen as his attempt to deny his helplessness in a real situation, for no matter how much he might protest, willynilly he would be brought to the Clinic and eventually to his sessions.

Another aspect of this defense was his denial of the lack of a penis in women; e.g., when playing with a doll he spoke of it indiscriminately as "he" or "she," pointing at it and insisting that it had a winkie. This was associated with his fear of castration as a retaliatory measure against him. (Weekly Reports Nos. 5, 6, 7.)

(Second Indexing): Further determinants of this denial were seen at a later stage of treatment when he once more denied in words that women have no penises. When the therapist told him that Andy knew very well that women do not have them, but that he thought that they had had them and then lost them, Andy later in that week evidenced a fantasy that if adults can take away his penis, they can also give him a bigger, better one. When this was verbalized to him, he replied that "ladies have bums and baby holes, they don't have winkies." Further elucidation revealed, however, that beneath this realistic assessment lay the fantasy that his mummy had once had a winkie but had given it to him when he was a little baby and that this fantasy served to deny his

anxiety about her possible castration of him. (Weekly Report No. 39.)

Ego: Defenses: Other Defensive Measures

DENIAL IN FANTASY

Denial in fantasy serves the devaluation of unpleasant reality, external or internal, by replacing it in games, verbally expressed or dramatized fantasies, daydreams, etc., which contain contrasting highly pleasurable or narcissistically gratifying content (e.g., "rescue" fantasies).

What was generally denied were his helplessness and smallness in an adult world. Although this was regarded as a normal pre-stage of defense at his developmental level, nevertheless the frequency and persistence of his usage are worth recording in order to follow later possible developments of the defense. One outstanding example was his frequent assertion of the supremacy of little tigers, etc., over large ones. (Weekly Reports Nos. 7, 10, 12.)

(Second Indexing): The frequency of this defensive measure diminished. The last example was seen in the last week of treatment. The arrangement was that he would be seen once a week after the Christmas holiday, and of course he had known this for some time. Nevertheless, during the last week he said that he would be seeing the therapist on practically every day of the week and this was followed by saying that he would see the therapist again when he was eight years old. This fantasy did not persist and he was well able to acknowledge the reality and to be in touch with his sadness about it. (Weekly Report No. 50.)

Ego: Defenses: Other Defensive Measures

DENIAL IN FANTASY (AND IDENTIFICATION)

Part of the identification with the father as an active person who drives lorries was used to defend against the anxiety aroused by father's being away from home one night each week driving his lorry. This anxiety was twofold: it concerned the possible loss of father and it also concerned the danger inherent in the opportunity thus given for Andy to be alone with mother. Both aspects of the anxiety were shown in his games of being the daddy who takes his baby with him when he goes driving—mother is left behind. This defense was used fairly frequently during that phase of treatment which coincided with the beginning of father's job as a lorry driver and also with various breaks in treatment. (Weekly Reports Nos. 23, 24, 27.)

CHAPTER 10

INSTINCTUAL

In this section are listed items of material brought by the child in treatment which were understood as expressions of instinctual demands and which were considered to be important for the understanding of the dynamic aspects of the patient's psychopathology. Since a great number of factors determine the material manifest in treatment, and its evaluation, subheadings had to be devised on different levels. These are ordered as follows:

1. Descriptive subheadings (in alphabetical order)—*Aggression* to *Scoptophilia*.

2. A set of headings grouped under *Zones of Excitation and Discharge* (or *Levels of Instinctual Development*), with a number of further subdivisions under each heading. For convenience this main heading is referred to as *Zones and Levels*.

3. Summaries of instinctual aspects.

The first two overlap to some extent, but not completely. It is left to the therapist to emphasize one or another aspect of the material according to his preference, and to place the text card describing the observed material in either the "descriptive" or the "zonal" section, and to cross-reference under the other relevant headings. Generally only one text card is made out for each item recorded, except where such a degree of overdetermination exists that a breaking down of the text contained in the main text card (under specific subheadings) seems indicated. In such a case the main text card is placed under a "descriptive" heading.

Text cards should contain:

(a) a description of the observed behavior, clearly stating the form in which it was expressed (e.g., verbally);

(b) the context in which it was brought by the patient, or the phase of treatment;

(c) the meaning as understood and as interpreted; and the patient's response to interpretation.

The "descriptive" headings contain instinctual manifestations of special interest. Both direct expressions and instinctual derivatives may be indexed here.

The *Zones and Levels* headings list the dynamic aspects of instinctual manifestations. They include the well-known component sexual instincts, but less regularly specified areas of erotogenicity may be indexed there using appropriate subheadings.

Text cards under zonal headings may be of three main kinds, viz.:

(a) statements of instinctual content, e.g., an oral aim;

(b) statements of an expression in terms of one level of an instinctual aim pertaining to another level, e.g., a phallic aim expressed in oral terms of "biting off." A distinction should also be made, for instance, between a phallic wish expressed in oral terms with accompanying phallic excitation, and the same fantasy expressed in oral terms with manifestations of accompanying excitation of the oral zone.

Therapists are also asked to state here failure to achieve an age-adequate level. Care should be taken to distinguish between developmental level and zone and, wherever possible, the zone or zones in which excitement is experienced should be stated.

The third (*Summary*) section was devised to cater for those cases where the instinctual aspects are of focal importance for the psychopathology, or are of special interest for the therapist. In this section are listed

(a) the development of material during the treatment (progressive and regressive) and the stage reached at the conclusion of treatment;

(b) general features of instinctual development (e.g., excessively high or low degrees of expression of aggressive impulses);

(c) relations between zones and levels during development (e.g., fixation, overlapping, regression); and

(d) relations between instincts and ego (e.g., respective strengths, ego control, id irruptions, efficiency of defenses, etc.).

Further subheadings are available for such aspects as *Passivity*. Negative instinctual aspects are also indexed, where a positive instinctual manifestation would normally be expected, but is diminished or absent.

Summary cards tend on the whole to be made at the conclusion of treatment.

The *Instinctual* section is at present undergoing extensive revision and reorganization.

INSTINCTUAL: Aggression

Cards are placed under this heading which refer to single behavioral instances of aggression, or habitual aggressive reactions, which are not entered under other headings in the Index.

An example of aggressive reaction to frustration was seen at the end of a session in which Andy had tried very hard to seduce the therapist into making a baby with him. His disappointment and rage were impulsively translated into kicking the therapist's face when the latter bent down to fix Andy's sandal.

On return from a lengthy break in treatment Andy said that he had thought the therapist was buried, because he was dead. Although interpretation was confined to his sadness at possible loss of love object, it was also understood as a possible death wish. (Weekly Report Nos. 12, 18.)

INSTINCTUAL: Bisexual Conflict

Under this heading should be placed cards describing manifestations of *conflicting tendencies,* e.g., instances of simultaneous, compromise, or alternating manifestations, as well as
any verbalization of the conflict. A number of alternative
headings are available for indexing bisexual conflict. If it is
mainly expressed in object relationship, the text should be
placed there, either under *Characteristics* (e.g., *Passive*); or
under the particular *Object* (e.g., father, mother, friend).
Manifestations of the bisexual wish (not showing conflict)
may be listed under other *Instinctual* headings, e.g., passive
sexual tendencies in boys under *Homosexuality;* and tomboy
or masculine fantasies or behavior in girls under *Phallic:
Penis Envy.*

The negative aspect of passivity (i.e., the inhibited aggression), often implied in bisexual manifestations, may be listed
under *Instinctual: Summary of Instinctual Aspects: Passivity.*

At one stage there was marked fluctuation in the transference
between Andy's passive and active wishes toward the therapist.
On one occasion he tried to seduce the therapist into lying beside
him on the couch, the therapist to play the feminine role. In the
same week he was much identified with the mother and when this
was interpreted he lay down on the couch, drew up his legs and
opened them, putting his hand over his penis. Following interpretation of his wish to do what mummy does in bed with daddy, he
denied this, but showed that his fear of castration had been
aroused. Nevertheless, at the next session he was again showing
his wish to play the female role in making babies. (Weekly Reports Nos. 8, 9, 12.)

INSTINCTUAL: Curiosity

Cards indexed should describe sexual curiosity, however
manifested.

Specific zonal subheadings may be given. This heading
should be distinguished from certain other headings dealing

with aspects of curiosity, e.g., *Instinctual: Scoptophilia* (referring to the obtaining of libidinal or aggressive gratification
from looking), and *Ego: Wish for Knowledge* (referring to
the thirst for knowledge, i.e., curiosity not specifically sexual,
not libidinized, and nearer to sublimation).

Permanent cross-references exist to *Ego: Wish for Knowledge, Instinctual: Scoptophilia,* and a number of symptoms
such as secretiveness, voyeurism, learning disturbances, and
tics.

Andy often referred to distant noises, e.g., the sound of a typewriter, and asked what it was, in the context of intercourse fantasies. Early in treatment he played with a miniature doll which
he called a lady, at first wanting to undress it to give her a wash,
then wanting to see the lady's knickers. He would later play with
another doll, constantly dressing and undressing it, wanting to see
her bum.

In the transference, following an interruption in treatment, he
wanted to know with whom the therapist had been, thinking it
was with another friend. His mother reported discovering him
involved in a game of doctors and patients with an older girl who
was feeling his penis. Andy referred to this as a game in which the
girl was testing him as the doctor does. (Weekly Reports Nos. 1,
2, 7, 15, 21.)

INSTINCTUAL: Exhibitionism

Cards listing a variety of manifestations may be placed here
(e.g., showing of body or parts of it; pleasure taken in, or fear
of, being looked at or photographed; manifestations of non-
bodily exhibitionism; inhibition of or conflict over exhibitionism).

Here again there are permanent cross-references to *Ego:
Restrictions of Ego Functions; Ego: Interests and Achieve-
ments; Symptoms;* and *Treatment Situation and Technique:
Activities and Behavior During Session.*

Andy had a need to show off, and this was mainly phallic, although there were remnants of anal exhibitionism in his wish to

be tested, i.e., examined as by a doctor, on the "bum." On several occasions he wished the therapist to accompany him to the lavatory. This was understood as a wish to exhibit, associated with a need to be reassured that his penis was intact. It was reported by the mother that when he used an adult phrase his grandparents were amused and this led Andy to repeat the phrase often to gain their admiration. (Weekly Reports Nos. 1, 4, 8.)

(Second Indexing): Sublimation of exhibitionism was seen later in his wish to be seen as the big boy who is polite to ladies and who can do things like going to the lavatory by himself; e.g., when we met anybody on the stairs, he stood aside to let them pass, always turning to the therapist afterwards to say, "I let that Mrs. pass, didn't I?" And he would be extremely pleased when the therapist complimented him on his good manners. (Weekly Report No. 41.)

INSTINCTUAL: Oedipal

Although largely an aspect of the development of object relationships, this heading has been retained under *Instinctual* since it denotes a well-defined and clinically described step and phase in libidinal development. Text cards placed under this heading should refer to the *incestuous wish.* (In other cases they are to be placed under *Object Relationships.*) The absence of manifestations of the oedipal phase where they would normally be expected should be particularly noted under this heading. Both positive oedipal manifestations and oedipal conflict are entered under this heading, but there is a separate subheading for *Negative Oedipal.*

Permanent cross-references are available to various aspects of *Object Relationships, Fantasies,* and assorted headings in the *Symptoms* section.

Following a phase in which either parent was wished for as partner, oedipal material was abundant in games and fantasies. Mother was the object of his libidinal desires, someone to be protected; father was feared as a castrator. Both relationships appeared in the transference. After several sessions in which he spoke of wolves, tigers, and monkeys attacking little wolves and tigers and several days on which he "shot" any men he met on the stairs, he played at opening and shutting his locker and later in the session spoke lovingly of his "sister baby" (actually a cousin). He flirted with the therapist and invited him to lie beside him on the couch. Interpretation of this wish to do to the therapist what daddy does to mummy in bed elicited a loving smile with an endearment "fuckie bogie." This was followed by his putting the locker keys up his jersey and when the likeness of the keys to his winkie was pointed out, he invited the therapist to go to bed once more. Father as castrator was seen in Andy's story of the little boy who met a gee-gee and the gee-gee bit him and the little boy said fuck and told the gee-gee get out—a healthier response than that of Little Hans. (Weekly Reports Nos. 3, 10, 11, 12.)

INSTINCTUAL: Oedipal

NEGATIVE OEDIPAL

This was a brief phase and was ushered in in treatment by Andy's identifying himself with a pussy which is hurt and is comforted by the big wolf (father in previous fantasies) who carries the pussy on his back. This was followed by a crashing game which was called "playing babbies" by Andy and in which the therapist was invited to join. He said that he had a babby inside his car, and this turned out to be an anal baby inside him. At the next session his play showed identification with the mother; when this was pointed out to him, he lay down on the couch, opened his legs, and put his hand on his penis. This was interpreted as his wish for the therapist to do to him what daddy does to mummy. He denied this, saying, "No, I'm not, give me your bleeding keys" and tried to open the locker but gave up very quickly and clutched at his penis, saying, "Oh me little winkie." (Weekly Report No. 12.)

INSTINCTUAL: Zones and Levels

ANAL

The heading *Anal* is to be used for all text cards for which no specific subheading has been listed. Permanent cross-references exist to *Ego: Defenses* (especially *Reaction Formation*),

Interests and Achievements, Sublimations, Fantasies, and symptoms of various types (compulsions, obsessions, rituals, ceremonials), disturbances manifested on the body relating to the anus and elimination, and disturbances of social behavior (such as messiness and obstinacy).

At the beginning of treatment anal drives and expressions were shown in messing activities, but also very soon Andy was able to verbalize his anal pleasure and aggression. There were many anal intercourse and conception fantasies. Anal drives were sometimes expressed via swearwords. During one session he wanted the therapist to play a game of crashing cars and animals together. When this was interpreted as his wish to make a baby, he put them into the wastepaper basket, saying he was putting them into the potty. When told that he thought he could make babies like jobbies, he rattled them about in the basket, said "Fuckie bogie" over them, then sat on the basket and grinned. At another session it was obvious from a game with moo-cows that smacking on the bottom produces babies. The making of plasticine animals represented anal babies, making him excited. He would yell "poo-poos" at them, squash them, and throw them about, and threaten to hit the therapist on his "bleeding bum."

At several sessions, after violent and exciting throwing games, he would play with a toy horse, dropping it repeatedly into a tumblerful of water and saying, "Plop, plop." The therapist was always invited to join him in this activity.

Various terms such as "Mr. Bum, Knick-Knick bottom, poo-poos" were used either lovingly or abusively. Speech contained a large anal element; he would excitedly pour out a string of "dirty words," and on one occasion he even looked as if he were defecating. (Weekly Reports Nos. 5, 6, 7, 9, 12, 21, 24.)

INSTINCTUAL: Zones and Levels

ANAL: Anal-Aggressive

The heading *Anal-Aggressive* includes *Anal-Sadistic.* However, the heading on the card may be more specific. The term *Anal-Aggressive* applies where the relationship is not predominantly libidinal and where the impulse is expressed either toward persons or things. *Anal-Sadistic,* in contrast, applies where the object relationship is predominantly to a person or persons, and shows an ambivalent admixture of love (e.g., in biting and kissing, whether simultaneous or in succession). If there is any doubt, *Aggressive* is preferred.

Anal-aggressive impulses were seen in his activities during sessions; e.g., calling pieces of plasticine "poo-poos" and then hurling them about the room, but he was also able to verbalize these impulses. He used swearwords as an expression of his anal aggressiveness, sometimes provocatively. Smacking on the bottom was a means of producing a baby and was a common component in his intercourse and conception fantasies.

There were hints at the defense of reaction formation against his anal aggression in his declaration, at a time when he was angry with the therapist, that the cars and animals must be nice and clean and he must wash them. (Weekly Reports Nos. 2, 6, 9, 14.)

(Second Indexing): Apart from the occasional use of the phrase "stinky bum" when he was angry during the latter part of the treatment, there were no anal-aggressive manifestations during sessions.

INSTINCTUAL: Zones and Levels

ANAL: Anal Smells

The heading *Anal Smells* is specific for the production of and interest in *anal* smells; e.g., flatus, making of chemical mixtures with emphasis on their disgusting or anal smell, smelling at people or their personal belongings with a libidinal anal bias. This should be distinguished from *Olfactory*, which is a broader and more general interest in smells and smelling (as seen in blind children).

These were referred to in various contexts. As a term of abuse Andy would tell the therapist or passers-by that they stink or were stinky poos and stinky bums. On other, nonaggressive, occasions, "stinky bum" was a term of endearment. The pleasure in anal smells was mingled with disgust. When in playing with a doll he would say the doll had done poo-poos and would wrinkle up his nose in disgust, this expression would rapidly alternate with one of delight. One day when playing at dropping toys in the water and saying "Plunk, plunk," he invited the therapist to join him. When this was interpreted as a wish for the therapist to admire his poo-poos, he excitedly ran toward the therapist and went through the motions of putting a napkin on him, saying delightedly, "Poo, you stink." This was understood as identification of the therapist with his beloved poo-poos. (Weekly Reports Nos. 9, 12, 22.)

INSTINCTUAL: Zones and Levels

ORAL: Oral-Aggressive

As with *Anal-Aggressive,* both sadistic and aggressive elements may be recorded under this heading.

Andy's mother reported that he often bit his three-year-old cousin and that he often bit the facecloth in his bath, shaking it as a puppy does. In sessions he bit most of the toys and the therapist. Swearwords were frequently used aggressively, although sometimes these were anal-aggressive derivatives expressed orally; e.g., at a time when he was angry with the therapist he addressed everybody rudely as "Mrs. Bum." (Weekly Reports Nos. 2, 3, 12, 16.)

INSTINCTUAL: Zones and Levels

ORAL: Speech

Cards placed here should describe the libidinized or inhibited function of speech. Permanent cross-references exist to *Ego: Language; Symptoms* (certain *Disturbances of Social Behavior;* and *Disturbances of Ego Functions: Speech*).

Speech is freely used for the expression of many instinctual ends; it is highly sexualized. Words, especially newly learned ones, are poured out in an excited, repetitive way and Andy derives much oral gratification from this. The most prominent instinctual expression is that of anal aggression; e.g., he has a kind of litany comprising the words and phrases "Fuck, fuckie, fuckie bogie, bleedin' ear'ole, blimey, poo-poo," which he repeats over and over again. On one such occasion he looked as if he were actually defecating—his face flushed and distorted, he was puffing through his nose and his arms were folded. (Weekly Report No. 7.)

INSTINCTUAL: Zones and Levels

PHALLIC

The term *Phallic* includes the clitoral zone. Permanent cross-references exist for a great variety of headings in the *Instinctual, Fantasies,* and *Symptoms sections.* Cross-referencing is of particular importance in regard to this heading for all phallic wishes expressed in oral or anal terms, and classified under those zonal headings.

Phallic drives were seen in behavior and verbalized wishes. In sessions Andy would often climb from one piece of furniture to another, jump to the ground from the couch, etc., and generally show an adventurous exploring spirit. On going downstairs he developed a game which consisted of launching himself into space, while holding the therapist's hand, wanting to jump further and further each day. It was as if he felt capable of flying, an omnipotent fantasy. His domineering attitude was particularly directed toward the mother, also the therapist in the transference. He was reported to have stood up to his grandfather when the latter was abusing Andy's mother, telling him not to shout at his mother so and leading the mother away by the hand. In games with toys there were many evidences of phallic drives—sticking pins in dolls, racing cars and trains, shooting with imaginary guns, driving lorries, flying aeroplanes.

Phallic excitement often followed activities and fantasies relating to his oedipal situation, and later in treatment this was combined with pleasure in demonstrating his ability to manage the whole process of using the W.C. properly by himself. He often used keys symbolically; e.g., when excited by an oedipal fantasy in the transference, he put the keys up his jersey. He frequently tried to master the art of opening the locked cupboard, insisting that he should do this and not the therapist. Tenderness as a phallic manifestation was shown in the games in which he played at being the father who takes his wife and children for runs in his lorry. He took care of the children (dolls), wrapping them up and wanting them to have a good view from the lorry. (Weekly Reports Nos. 5, 7, 12, 24.)

INSTINCTUAL: Zones and Levels

PHALLIC: Castration Anxiety (and Castration Wish)

Material indexed here contains instances of directly expressed castration anxiety. The heading *Castration Wish* refers to the wish to castrate others. Cards showing the wish to be castrated are placed elsewhere under *Phallic*. Other subheadings refer to feelings of being castrated, penis envy, etc.

This was first verbalized in a story of a little boy meeting a gee-gee who bit the little boy who said "fuck" and told the gee-gee to get out. After telling this story Andy stood up and held his penis saying that he would put a pin in his winkie, then changed his mind and said he would put a pin in the therapist's winkie. Another reference the following day to somebody putting a pin in a little boy's winkie was immediately followed by a desire to urinate, interpreted as his need to reassure himself that his winkie was still working, as he feared it had been hurt.

On another occasion the interpretation of his wish to be the mummy in bed with daddy produced the response of his clutching his penis and exclaiming, "Oh, me little winkie." When this was interpreted as the fear of losing his winkie if his wish to be the mummy came true, he said that the bleeding tiger will cut it off, but he would not let it.

A frequent fantasy at one stage was of a big wolf up a tree who would jump down and bite a little wolf "on the ear-ole or the belly or the winkie." Interpretation of the little wolf as Andy who feared somebody would hurt him in this way brought the response: "I wouldn't let him." On this occasion the linkage between the fear of being castrated and the wish to castrate was seen in his statement that the big wolf was up the tree because Andy had chased him up there. (Weekly Reports Nos. 4, 10, 12.)

INSTINCTUAL: Summary of Instinctual Aspects

AGGRESSION

Cards under this heading give a summary picture for patients in whose psychopathology aggression plays a prominent part. It is desirable that the text of the card should cover

(a) the quantitative aspect of aggressive trends as such (excessively strong or very low) and in their relation to the ego (respective strength, control, irruption, efficiency of defenses, etc.);

(b) the main areas of direct or indirect expression (verbalized, in behavior, fantasies, defenses, symptoms, affects, and object relations);

(c) the zonal aspect in regard to both aim and mode of expression (i.e., as an aggressive admixture to particular component sexual instincts);

(d) the development and changes during treatment;

(e) assessment at the conclusion of treatment. Statements in the text of the card may refer to other cards listing pertinent material.

This drive was very strong and much of the aggression was free-floating and readily available; zonally, perhaps because of the stage of his development, all levels were represented in Andy's behavior, e.g., in biting, throwing and wanting to stick pins in inanimate objects and therapist. Aggression was also readily available as a reaction to anxiety. Frustration also aroused it, and the aggressive response was usually expressed immediately, either in action or verbally.

Recently there have been changes in the direction of efforts at control. (Weekly Reports Nos. 1, 2, 12, 15, 19, 21, 22.)

(Second Indexing): In the latter stages of treatment, the expression of aggression was more in words than in action—a reversal of the earlier balance. (Weekly Report No. 45.)

INSTINCTUAL: Summary of Instinctual Aspects

OVERLAPPING OF PHASES (NORMAL)

This heading covers what is sometimes described as "chaotic instinctual development." It is to be distinguished from (a) the normal overlapping of instinctual levels, and from (b) fixation, which refers to a specific developmental phase or zone.

At the time of indexing Andy is regarded as predominantly a phallic boy, but at the beginning of treatment there was much overlapping of anal and phallic drives, with occasionally oral-anal admixtures.

One pleasurable activity which combined oral and anal pleasures was a game in which he dropped a toy horse into a tumblerful of water, picked it out and sucked it. This was repeated again and again with manifest enjoyment. Anal messing was often accompanied by biting and sucking. Many phallic manifestations were interlinked with anal ones, or were expressed in anal terms; e.g., a crashing game with cars to make a baby would be combined with fantasies of making a baby anally.

Washing games were a mixture of anal and phallic phenomena. He would be in charge of the doll being washed, examining its winkie and making it urinate, but the washing was usually a messy affair and quickly led to the expression of anal-aggressive impulses, but also phallic excitement. At one session he washed a doll, then pulled up her skirt, saying, "Let's look at her bum, stick a pin in her bum, take her clothes off." This followed on an invitation to the therapist, in preference to the mother, to help him urinate; i.e., it was seen as a combination of his anal passivity in relation to the phallic mother and phallic activity in relation to the anal mother. The response to the interpretation of this was excited splashing of water and a renewed desire to urinate. (Weekly Reports Nos. 3, 5, 8, 9, 13, 15.)

(Second Indexing): Overlapping was not at all in evidence during the last months of treatment, and he was seen as firmly in the phallic phase.

CHAPTER 11

OBJECT RELATIONSHIPS

This section provides for the indexing of the child's ability to relate to objects (persons or nonhuman objects), the manner in which he does so, and the objects to which he relates. For cards in this section any source of information may be used (referral agents, patient, observation outside treatment by therapist or others, analytic material, etc.).

Object relationships cards are to be found under four main subheadings.

1. Capacity for Object Relationships
2. Characteristics
3. Objects (i.e., the relationship with the specific object)
4. Summary cards

Aspects of the child's relationship to the therapist are placed under *Treatment Situation and Technique: Relationship to Therapist* or *Treatment Situation and Technique: Transference.* Fantasied object relationships are placed under *Fantasies* wherever possible.

Object Relationships

capacity for object relationships

Cards placed under this heading give an assessment of the capacity for making object relationships, especially of the negative aspects (such as impairment, or age inadequacy of this capacity).

Special subheadings refer to the inability to cathect objects, and the inability to introject objects, as well as to limitations in the capacity for object relationships of various sorts.

Andy shows a high capacity for object relationships, his choice being widely based (adults, other children, and animals). He showed early his faithfulness to chosen objects; e.g., his mother overheard him talking to a puppy which had in fact disappeared several months before. He used token objects (e.g., teddy bears and dolls) as aids in maintaining a link with the object.

Object Constancy. He developed consideration and concern for his love objects during the course of treatment, e.g., his protective attitude toward his mother during the course of a quarrel between her and his grandfather and also his quietness when told of his father's headaches. (Interview with mother and child [Chapter 3], Weekly Reports Nos. 7, 12, 27.)

OBJECT RELATIONSHIPS: Characteristics

AGGRESSIVE

Cards placed under *Characteristics* should refer to more than one object and should give a descriptive summary picture. When the type of relationship is limited to one person or one group of people (e.g., friends), the card is placed under a more specific subheading (e.g., *Object Relationships: Objects: Self,* or *Other Persons,* etc.).

The subheadings in the section *Characteristics* are meant to be descriptive. They refer to aspects of object relationships manifested in behavior, whether in action or by speech. The dynamic, structural, and etiological aspects should, however, be worked out in the text.

There are permanent cross-references for cards under this heading to *Symptoms: Disturbances of Social Behavior,* in particular: *Defiance, Destructiveness, Negativism, Provocativeness, Rages and Temper Tantrums,* etc. There are also cross-references to the *Instinctual* section, e.g., *Aggression, Passivity.*

This was a feature of Andy's relationships complained of at referral, particularly with reference to other children. It is thought that his favored position in his family situation as the much-loved only child and grandchild (of paternal grandparents) contributed to this, but also his naturally assertive personality was a contributory factor. Strong anal-sadistic trends formed the instinctual background to his aggressiveness, and were stimulated by the grandfather in his play with Andy. (Interview with mother and child [Chapter 3], Weekly Reports Nos. 2, 4.)

OBJECT RELATIONSHIPS: Characteristics

PROVOCATIVE, SEDUCTIVE

The specific heading *Provocative, Seductive* has been devised for such normal manifestations as the seductiveness of girls at the height of the oedipal phase who invite men to become their partners. This seductiveness differs quantitatively from seductiveness as a symptom. When the behavior is regarded as symptomatic, it should be indexed under Symptoms: *Disturbances of Sexual Behavior: Seductiveness.*

The characteristic was manifested early in treatment and was seen in the transference as relating to the paternal grandfather and the mother. Much of the provocativeness was a testing out, to see how much the object could stand of Andy's aggression without deserting him. It was also a means of reducing his anxiety about his own aggression by stimulating aggression in the object. (Weekly Reports Nos. 1, 2, 3, 4, 6.)

OBJECT RELATIONSHIPS: Objects

Material indexed under the broad heading *Objects* should describe the relationship to all persons or things that play an important role in the child's life as recipients of cathexis, as revealed either by the analytic material or from outside sources of information. Cards should describe the relationship at the time of referral and at the time of indexing, the aspects of the previous history of this relationship relevant to the understanding of the case, and the nature of and reasons

for the changes in the relationship during the course of treatment, if any. The analytic understanding of the relationship
should be given wherever possible.

Identifications are considered to be an outcome of object
relationships. Cards stressing the relationship and mentioning a resulting identification, and meeting the above requirements should be placed here, and cross-references made to
Ego: Identification, or to *Ego: Defenses: Defense Mechanisms: Identification.* Cards highlighting the identification
aspect should be placed under the appropriate one of these
last two headings.

When a card describes a relationship to an object in the
past or present about which no material appears in treatment,
or in which no changes occur attributable to treatment, this
card should not be placed here. Such cards should be placed
under the appropriate heading in *General Case Material.*

Relationships to lost or absent objects should be indexed
under the appropriate *Objects* subheading (e.g., mother,
father, uncle, aunt, etc.), and a cross-reference made to the
special heading referring to relationships to absent, lost, or
fantasied objects.

OBJECT RELATIONSHIPS: Objects

MOTHER

Mother is the object of Andy's ambivalence. He frequently tells
her he loves her and is her little darling, but she quickly becomes
the object of his hate and aggression whenever the possibility
arises of being left for any length of time. During treatment she
has been seen as a need-satisfier but also as his love object in the
oedipal situation. She appears also as a partner in a sadomasochistic
relationship in which she apologizes after a quarrel between them
and there is then a loving reconciliation. (Weekly Reports Nos.
1, 2, 3, 5, 6, 12, 18, 19, 22.)

(Second Indexing): Following on his firm establishment in the
oedipal situation, he showed signs of being able to move out toward his age peers. In fact, when he went to nursery school imme-

diately following the end of intensive treatment, he was able to part from his mother with ease, thus indicating the resolution of his ambivalence to her. (Weekly Reports Nos. 47, 48.)

OBJECT RELATIONSHIPS: Objects

FATHER

Father is a feared, loved, and admired person, feared because he might castrate Andy if he knew of Andy's wish to make babies with mother, i.e., as the oedipal rival. He was loved and wanted as a possible partner in the making of anal babies—this pre-oedipally, and also fleetingly in a negative oedipal sense. He is admired as the big, strong daddy who drives lorries and aeroplanes. Andy's love and concern for his father are shown in his willingness to be quiet when father has a headache and in the ready identification with him as the provider for the family. (Weekly Reports Nos. 2, 3, 4, 5, 7, 10, 12, 23, 24, 27.)

OBJECT RELATIONSHIPS: Objects

SELF

Cards under this heading should show

(1) how the child evaluates himself, including his body (e.g., wholly good, wholly bad, or part good and part bad), i.e., the state of the narcissistic cathexis of the self;

(2) the role he ascribes to himself in his object relationships (e.g., as obedient, as a follower, leader, etc.), and whether or not he in fact plays this role;

(3) the origins of the foregoing features (e.g., conflicting, double or multiple identifications, etc.).

Andy values himself highly, i.e., narcissistic cathexis of the self is high. Although for the most part he sees himself as good, at times he sees himself as bad and can volunteer the information that he is a bad boy. In his object relationships he ascribes the leading role to himself and any real contradiction of this is met with fury; e.g., if his mother insists that he must do something she wishes him to do, he becomes angry and obstinate; when he says, "I don't want to," that should be an end of it. The origins of these features seems to be the fact that he is highly cathected by parents and grandparents, together with identification with the paternal grandfather. He easily accepts admiration from strangers (e.g., staff at the Clinic) as if it were his indisputable right, because it fits in with his picture of himself. (Weekly Reports Nos. 1, 4, 5, 7; Therapist's observations, not in reports.)

OBJECT RELATIONSHIPS: Objects

FRIENDS

Andy was reported to have one special friend, a boy, before treatment. He played with him without his usual aggressiveness. Since moving to the new flat he has acquired other friends, mostly older than himself. With one of these, a girl of four, he plays sexual games. Another, a boy of five, is greatly admired by Andy. (Interview with mother and child [Chapter 3], Weekly Report No. 21; Mother's statement, not in reports.)

OBJECT RELATIONSHIPS: Objects

GRANDPARENTS

Before treatment there was an intense relationship between Andy and his paternal grandfather. This man is a very disturbed person and the relationship was a sadomasochistic one; e.g., they had mutual hitting and pinching games in which Andy was encouraged to hurt paternal grandfather as much as he could. Andy was very fond of him, but kept well away from grandmother (nana) whom he openly said he disliked. The reason for this is not yet clear, although it is thought to be a possible split in his ambivalent feelings for mother. (Interview with mother and child [Chapter 3], Interview with parents [Chapter 4]; Weekly Reports Nos. 1, 3, 4; Mother's statement, not in reports.)

OBJECT RELATIONSHIPS: Objects

OTHER PERSONS, ADULTS

With adults Andy's capacity for relationships was very high and these were of mixed types; e.g., with adults in the Clinic, particularly in the waiting room, he related easily, sometimes in a specially appropriate way, at other times aggressively. With the therapist there was a rapid establishment of a relationship in which he freely expressed feelings of all kinds. (Therapist's observations, not in reports; Mother's statement, not in reports; Weekly Report No. 9.)

OBJECT RELATIONSHIPS: Objects

OTHER PERSONS, CHILDREN

Andy had a sadomasochistic relationship with a boy cousin (G.) whom he used to bite and hit. The cousin used not to retaliate, but later did so and Andy became afraid of him. Nevertheless, Andy still insisted on visiting G., although he knew he would be hit. Later still in treatment he and G. have become able to play together without too much quarreling, although G. seems to be the leader in the relationship. (Weekly Reports Nos. 2, 22; Mother's statement, not in reports.)

OBJECT RELATIONSHIPS: Objects

INANIMATE OBJECTS

Andy uses inanimate objects freely as substitutes for human objects, either for loving or aggressive purposes. During treatment he took home a teddy bear from the Clinic and his mother says he will not be parted from it at nighttime. When she asked him where it had come from, he said it was his friend's (the therapist). (Weekly Reports Nos. 2, et seq.; Mother's statement, not in reports.)

OBJECT RELATIONSHIPS: Objects

ANIMALS

Andy was very fond of a pup which he had when he was about two, but together they created much noise in the house with their "quarreling," as mother called it, so that the grandparents got rid of the dog while Andy was away on holiday. He made no immediate reference to it on his return, but several weeks later was overheard addressing the missing dog, asking it if it had been away down the road. He frequently expresses the wish to have a pussy and a puppy, but his mother reports that he is afraid of them and will avoid them if possible. (Interview with mother and child [Chapter 3], Weekly Reports Nos. 18, 23.)

(Second Indexing): During the course of treatment he acquired two hamsters. They were rarely referred to during treatment, as was his budgerigar, although his mother reported that he was very fond of them. (Weekly Report No. 38.)

CHAPTER 12

FANTASIES

Here appear fantasies of the child which are brought during treatment by verbal or other means (e.g., drawing, dramatization, etc.) and which play an important role in the analysis or were unusual in their content.

In the *Fantasy* section we distinguish *characteristics* from fantasy *content* classified according to its manifest theme. This section is at present being substantially revised.

FANTASIES: Characteristics

ABUNDANCE OF

The subheadings in the section *Characteristics* contain the typical characteristics of the fantasy production of the patient. These include quantitative (abundance, paucity) as well as qualitative (e.g., sadistic) factors. Cards under these headings do not contain the content of fantasies, but they may have cross-references to the relevant manifest themes. Where possible the underlying cause for the specific characteristic should be given.

There are many fantasies, freely expressed, mainly anal-aggressive and oedipal, but widely ranging over Andy's entire inner life. Some of the fantasies are verbalized, but the majority are acted.

(Second Indexing): There was a diminution of fantasies during the last few months of treatment.

Fantasies: Characteristics

FORM

Fantasies were sometimes expressed in stories, often in games.

Fantasies: Characteristics

FUNCTION OF

The two principal functions so far ascertained are discharge of impulses (mainly aggressive) and defensive, particularly to deny unwanted affect or reality.

Fantasies: Characteristics

NATURE OF

The commonest trait of Andy's fantasies was aggression, with himself either the attacker or the attacked. It was associated frequently with castration fear, castration of others, death wishes and sadistic intercourse.

Fantasies: Manifest Themes

BEING ATTACKED

The text or content of conscious fantasies only are indexed under what the therapist judges to be the main manifest theme. The therapist is asked to list subsidiary themes as well, if these appear to be important.

The manifest theme card should contain

(1) the content (text) of the fantasy; (2) the context in which the fantasy appeared if this is relevant; (3) how the fantasy was understood and interpreted (i.e., its latent meaning).

If the fantasy was understood or partly understood by the therapist, but not interpreted at the time of its appearance, this should be noted.

If the fantasy has been mainly or wholly expressed in action rather than been verbalized, and the therapist wishes to stress this aspect, the content of the activity and its latent meaning may be indexed in the *Treatment Situation and Technique* section, and a cross-reference card to the appropriate *Fantasy* heading should be made.

At one phase in treatment Andy spoke often of a big wolf up a tree which would jump down and bite the little wolf on the ear'ole or on the belly or on the winkie. The wolf did these things because he wanted to, but gradually the story changed to the wolf's *wish* to attack the little wolf being thwarted because the little wolf would not let him. Finally, the big wolf was up the tree because Andy had chased him there.

Context: castration fear associated with the wish to make babies formed a large part of the material at this time. Interpretation of the castration fear led to the development of the story into one in which Andy's wish to castrate father was expressed. (Weekly Report No. 10.)

FANTASIES: Manifest Themes

BEING BITTEN

Andy told the therapist a story: "Once upon a time a little boy went for a walk down a road and he met a gee-gee and the gee-gee bit him and the little boy said fuck and told the gee-gee get out."

Context: efforts were being made to get him a bedroom of his own. His anxiety lest his mother would not be available when he would awake was being interpreted. The gee-gee had recently been identified as Andy himself, but now seemed also to represent father.

The story was repeated the following week with an addition— he held his penis and said he would put a pin in his winkie, then changed his mind and said he would put a pin in the therapist's winkie.

The fantasy was understood as his fear of castration by the father in the oedipal situation and his efforts to defy the castrator by biting him. Interpretation was made in stages:

1. Identifying the little boy as Andy, who does not like being bitten. His response was to bite the toy gee-gee.

2. His fear of being bitten arises from his wish to bite. His

response was aggressive behavior, followed by self-punishment in the form of bumping his head, interpreted as his hurting himself for fear of hurting somebody else.

3. Specifically that he was afraid that his daddy would hurt his winkie, but reassurance was given about this danger. (Weekly Reports Nos. 3, 4.)

FANTASIES: Manifest Themes

BEING COMFORTED BY THE AGGRESSOR

When Andy came into the treatment room one day he fell back against the couch and slid down to the floor, saying that the little pussy was falling on his bottom, the little pussy has hurt his bottom, the little pussy is crying, poor little pussy. But the big wolf comes along and says "Poor little pussy" and picks him up and carries him on his back and the little pussy is all right.

Context: Castration fear material was prominent, as was his aggressive behavior directed at the therapist. This behavior was linked with his disappointment in the therapist for not making a baby with him. Although the fantasy was understood as an attempt to deal with castration fear by making the threatening father into a benevolent one in the oedipal situation, it was not interpreted as such, the therapist preferring that Andy's wish to have a baby should be the focus of interpretation at that stage, although the two themes were linked together in interpretation later. (Weekly Report No. 12.)

FANTASIES: Manifest Themes

CHILDREN SLEEPING

Andy told a story illustrated by toy animals. He said the gee-gee and the baby moo-cow were going for a walk down a red road to a red park. He instructed the therapist to cradle the moo-cow in his arms while he himself did the same with the gee-gee, saying, "Go to sleep, little one." He put the gee-gee down on the table and placed the mother moo-cow beside it, but with a piece of fencing between them, saying, "And the mummy sleeps there."

Context: the mother was making arrangements for a separate bedroom for him and his anxiety about not seeing her if he should awake at night was being interpreted.

The red road and the red park were not understood (? mother's genital), but the remainder of the fantasy was an enactment of being cared for by the mother at bedtime. The function of the fantasy was to assure himself of his mother's nearness. No interpretation was made, but the therapist commented on the fact that each animal slept in its own room and the mummy slept near the baby in case he should be frightened during the night. (Weekly Report No. 3.)

FANTASIES: Manifest Themes

THE INJURED FATHER

At one time a favorite game was to play at being the daddy who drives a lorry and takes his babies (therapist and dolls) with him. Sometimes in this role he lay down on the couch, screwed up his face, saying, "Daddy has a bad head. Daddy hurt his head on the lorry. Daddy crashed his lorry, he isn't feeling well."

Context: Father had started a new job which entailed his being away from home one night each week. Andy's games were mostly in identification with this job, but he always took his babbas with him. He had been antagonistic toward the therapist, especially about week-end separations, but denied this as a transference from father.

Fantasy was understood as his death wishes directed against the father, defended against by denial and identification. Also contained in it was concern for the father, who really was having headaches at that time. It was the concern which was first interpreted, but this was then linked with his dislike of father's being away from home. The response was to tell the therapist to shut up. (Weekly Report No. 27.)

CHAPTER 13

SUPEREGO

A detailed account of the considerations relevant to the classification of superego material in the index has been given elsewhere, and will not be repeated here (Sandler et al., 1962). The cards presented in the case indexed here sample only a very few of the available headings in the *Superego* section (and this applies equally to all the other sections). The reader may be interested in comparing the material quoted here with the headings and illustrative cards presented in the previously published paper on the *Superego*.

SUPEREGO: Characteristics

SUPPORTIVE AND ADEQUATE

The headings grouped under *Characteristics* apply to statements referring to characteristics of the superego organization functioning as a structure or as a preautonomous superego schema (cf. Sandler, 1960). Where the superego is still in its preautonomous state, its characteristics will merge with features of authority figures in the child's object world, but will not necessarily be identical with them.

Etiological factors should be indicated in the text (e.g., particularly severe conflict over habit training, feeding; conflicts over temporary regression or over aggression).

Some indication should be given of the degree to which the characteristics are present.

Cards should indicate the particular impulses tolerated or not tolerated, as the case may be.

The heading *Supportive and Adequate* applies to material indicating that the superego provides a sufficient degree of security and well-being appropriate for age-adequate independence and adjustment to reality.

Because of the early stage of development of the superego which is functioning preautonomously, it provides a sufficient degree of security and well-being; e.g., early in treatment there was no apparent anxiety about his considerable aggressiveness. This is becoming modified as anxiety is developing and there is now more interplay between anxiety and the supportiveness of the superego.

SUPEREGO: Sources

OBJECT SOURCES

The material indexed here relates to the particular objects in the environment of the child whose perceived characteristics enter into the presuperego schema and into the superego. The child's perception of the objects may, of course, be influenced in a number of ways, e.g., by projection and idealization.

The main object sources discernible are the paternal grandfather, the mother, and the father.

The grandfather is the source from which is derived a degree of freedom from guilt and anxiety about his aggression. The mother is seen as the source from which is derived his budding altruism (mainly under the influence of his loving oedipal feelings for her). The father was seen as the punishing authority figure in the oedipal situation and also served as a model through identification with his activity. (Interview with mother and child [Chapter 3], Interview with parents [Chapter 4], Weekly Reports Nos. 2, 3, 8, 20, 24.)

Superego: Sources

INSTINCTUAL SOURCES

Cards indexed here indicate the way in which the child's own instinctual drives and their derivatives are deployed in the superego, e.g., the reinforcement of the child's superego by his own aggression.

Andy's aggression seems to reinforce the superego. This may be seen in his attitude to dolls which in fantasy represent himself and other children. He scolds them for being naughty and dirty, for doing wee-wee and poos, for stinking. This leads to harsh treatment of the dolls, and they are often smacked or even thrown at the wall or on the floor. This could be seen as a pre-stage in superego formation. (Weekly Reports Nos. 22, 24.)

Superego

CONTENTS ACTIVATING THE SUPEREGO SYSTEM

Cards indexed here should specify the instinctual impulse, fantasy, affect, and/or the activity which typically activates the superego system. Unconscious content should be distinguished as far as possible from conscious content. Contents are included when they also lead to the anticipation of a reaction by external authority figures (e.g., masturbation, looking, oedipal strivings, competing, being successful, etc.). There are permanent cross-references for cards under this heading to *Ego: Anxiety, Reaction to, Ego: Defenses, Fantasies,* and to other subsections in the *Superego* section (*Ego Response, Regulation of the Feeling of Well-Being*).

Aggression, particularly anal aggression, and oedipal strivings typically activate the preautonomous superego system, although the anal impulses first have to be carried into action before the prohibitive and punishing aspects of the (preautonomous) super-ego become active.

Oedipal strivings, as shown in fantasies, have come almost invariably to produce fear of castration by father. (Weekly Reports Nos. 3, 6.)

SUPEREGO: Ego Response
PROVOCATION OF PUNISHMENT

The subsection relating to *Ego Response* contains many different headings. Ideally it should include all the aspects of the ego's response to tension with internal or external authority, but for convenience we include only those headings which are specially relevant to the consideration of superego functioning, while others may be found in the various subsections of *Ego,* particularly *Ego: Defenses,* and *Ego: Anxiety, Reaction to.*

The material entered under the various *Ego Response* headings refers to the wish to please, or the fear of or the need to control, internal or external authority. A note should be made of whether or not the response follows an irruption of a forbidden impulse (in act or in fantasy), whether the response is predominantly autoplastic or alloplastic, and the degree of sexualization. The underlying affect should be indicated where possible.

The specific subheading *Provocation of Punishment* calls for a statement of the way in which the provocation serves to reduce tension with inner or outer authority. It should also include attempts to reduce this tension by means of the substitution of lesser offenses (e.g., certain delinquent acts). Forms of moral masochism which involve provocation should be indexed here.

He sometimes deals with his aggression by behaving provocatively, thus inviting punishment from his mother. In fact, the use of certain swearwords at one time inevitably provoked smacking by his mother. (Weekly Reports Nos. 1, 2, 3, 6.)

SUPEREGO: Ego Response
SELF-PUNISHMENT: Bodily Damage

The headings which relate to the various forms of self-punishment refer to the existence of tendencies of self-damage or self-punishment where this results from tension with inner or outer authority. Under *Bodily Damage* are included acts or accidents brought about consciously or unconsciously by the child. We also include the development and exacerbation of bodily symptoms for purposes of self-punishment.

This is most frequently seen as a result of tension with an external authority figure. For example, he bumped himself down on the floor when angry with the therapist about an unwelcome interpretation. The external authority is often represented in his fantasies. (Weekly Reports Nos. 16, 21.)

SUPEREGO: Ego Response

DEFIANCE

This refers to deliberate disregard, disobedience, rejection of or rebellion against internal or external authority.

Andy's defiance is often seen in the treatment situation when the therapist has to forbid certain activities (e.g., pulling at the wash-hand basin and towel rail). At times it occurred to such a degree that physical restraint had to be used. In fantasies he always defies the authority figure who is seen to be threatening him, e.g., in the story of the gee-gee who bit the little boy, the little boy said fuck and told the gee-gee to get out. (Weekly Reports Nos. 3, 4.)

SUPEREGO: Ego Response

FEAR OF PUNISHMENT

The child's fear of punishment may be reality-based or distorted to a varying degree by fantasies and defense mechanisms such as projection and displacement. The content of the child's fear should be described as far as possible (e.g., fears of being deserted, of physical illness, of bodily damage, of retaliation in kind, of loss of love, of criticism, etc.). A statement should be made as to whether this fear is manifest or latent.

His fear of punishment is latent in fantasies related to oedipal strivings. The punishment takes the form of bodily damage, usually castration. But on the whole there is remarkably little fear of punishment for his aggression. (Weekly Reports Nos. 3, 4.)

SUPEREGO: Ego Response

AFFECTIVE STATES: Remorse

The heading *Affective States* is used when the therapist wishes to highlight the emotional state in the child. Cards should contain the evidence on which the inference of the particular affective response is based (e.g., verbalization, motor behavior, facial expression, reactions to interpretation, etc.). If the ideational content rather than the affective state is to be stressed, then the material should be entered under other headings.

It was only after some time in treatment that Andy ever expressed remorse for his aggressive acts, and then only rarely. On one occasion he had kicked the therapist and almost immediately after said he was sorry and offered to "kiss it better." (Therapist's observation, not in reports.)

SUPEREGO: Regulation of the Feeling of Well-being

Cards placed under this heading contain material referring to the influence, or lack of influence, of authority figures (including introjects) upon the child's feelings of well-being and self-esteem. Cards should show in this connection the motives for the child's authority-oriented behavior, and also the extent to which this behavior is effective in regard to the regulation of well-being. It is not sufficient here to speak of "guilt feelings," but an attempt should be made to break these down into specific components. A distinction should be made, for example, between such factors as: the gaining of a feeling of omnipotence through identification with admired objects, or its opposite, the feeling of worthlessness which can arise from a lack of such identification; the loss or gain of love from the object (we include here loss of the object); the experience or avoidance of physical hurt; retaliation or reward in kind; losing or gaining a penis or its equivalent; praising or condemnation; shaming or admiring; and other punishments or rewards (e.g., gifts vs. deprivations).

The degree of reality or fantasy in the child's anticipations should be indicated.

Andy is a well-loved child and derives large narcissistic supplies from parents and grandparents. The principal motivation in the superego development is largely to earn praise and admiration, but also (minimally) fear of loss of love.

Under the impetus of the oedipal attachment to mother, and through his identification with the omnipotently active father, he has developed a loving, protective attitude to the mother; e.g., on one occasion when the mother and grandfather were quarreling, Andy told the grandfather not to shout at his mother like that and led her away by the hand.

This example also shows the breaking down of the influence of the grandfather, who was overpermissive toward Andy's aggression. This overpermissiveness had led to a relative lack of anxiety in him about his aggression, but under the other influence mentioned above, Andy makes tentative efforts at control of his aggression. (Weekly Reports Nos. 4, 12, 22.)

Superego: Extent of Organization and Structuralization

Any illustrative material relevant to stages or processes of superego development should be indexed here. Cards should give a picture of the state of superego development and also indicate changes during the course of treatment.

Where external persons are habitually used as authority figures an attempt should be made to differentiate between the tendencies to use persons and institutions as (1) externalization of introjects (externalization of superego); (2) replacements for introjects; (3) as real figures of authority who are relatively independent of the introjects.

By organization of the superego is meant the extent to which aspects of the authority figures and ego responses and functions are coordinated and integrated (irrespective of whether introjection of authority and consequent establishment of the superego as an autonomous structure has taken place). By structuralization of the superego is meant the extent to which the superego functions autonomously, i.e., the extent to which external authority has been introjected.

There is very little structuralization of the superego, as external authority has been little or not at all introjected. Thus, although it would appear on the surface that prohibition of messing has become internalized (as in the care with which he lifts the toilet seat before urinating and his scrupulous avoidance of dribbling), he nevertheless messed freely at home and in treatment, especially at the beginning of treatment.

However, some superego aspects have been taken over, particularly generosity and sharing; e.g., if he has sweets he often offers them to other children and adults (including the therapist) in the waiting room. His mother said that she has always encouraged him to share what he has with others.

He also showed a spontaneous expression of remorse after attacking the therapist. He usually needs an external authority figure to reinforce prohibitions. (Weekly Reports Nos. 8, 9; Therapist's observations, not in reports.)

(Second Indexing): Later in treatment there was evidence of internalization through identification in his politeness to passersby. Although this was spontaneous, he still needed external approval of his behavior and when this was given, on one occasion he said, "Sometimes I'm quite good, aren't I?" (Weekly Report No. 41.)

CHAPTER 14

SYMPTOMS

The term *Symptom* is used very broadly in compiling index cards. It is used to cover descriptions of behavior which the referral agency, therapist, supervisor, and Index Committee consider to be of possible psychopathological interest. The *Symptom* section is undergoing extensive revision and the present classification is a temporary one.

Both referral and transitory symptoms are listed; whenever possible, past symptoms are also recorded. The headings in the symptom section are for the most part descriptive, and although an attempt has been made to classify descriptions of specific, small units of behavior, there is considerable variation in the size of units described on the cards, some categories being much more inclusive than others.

As far as possible, symptom cards should comply with the following requirements:

1. A statement should be made whether the symptom is

(a) a referral symptom, i.e., complaints made by mother (or others) irrespective of the emphasis by the referral agent. These should include statements not given as an immediate reason for referral if it is seen later that the material to which they refer appears to be symptomatic in character;

(b) emerged symptoms (i.e., those which were noticed during treatment). These are psychopathological features which are found during treatment to have been present at the time

175

of referral but which had not been mentioned. They may be culled from various sources;

(c) transitory symptoms (symptoms appearing during treatment). These may be either new symptoms, or may have been symptoms in the patient's past life (before referral) but had ceased by the time the patient was referred for treatment. Pieces of behavior that can be understood as transference phenomena and are solely confined to the treatment should not be listed as transitory symptoms, but recorded in the section *Treatment Situation and Technique;*

(d) past symptoms (symptoms reported by any source as having existed in earlier years but not at the time of referral).

2. A full description of the symptom, as given by external informants and as observed during treatment, should be recorded. An indication should be given of the places where the symptom generally appeared (at home, at school, etc.); when first noticed; reality factors associated with onset; frequency of occurrence; and the source of information.

3. Etiological factors elicited in treatment should be fully stated; underlying conflicts; structural and dynamic aspects. Interpretations given and their effect should be fully noted.

4. Eventual changes in the symptom during or resulting from treatment should be recorded. The phase of treatment in which the change occurred should be noted.

There are eight main subgroups of *Symptom* headings.

1. Fears and Phobias
2. Compulsions, Obsessions, Rituals, Ceremonials
3. Disorders of Affect
4. Disturbances Manifested on the Body
5. Disturbances of Social Behavior
6. Disturbances of Sexual Behavior
7. Disturbances of Ego Functions
8. General Features of the Patient's Symptomatology

A number of symptoms lend themselves to listing under more than one main heading. In such cases the full text is given on one card and cross-reference cards are placed under the relevant headings.

If a symptom includes another symptom (i.e., a composite symptom), it is desirable that two text cards should be made for it. For example, a sleeping disturbance may be found to imply a fear of dying, of the dark, or of being murdered, and separate cards should be made for the sleeping disturbance (giving a full description of the disturbance, and mentioning the underlying fear as one of the determinants), and for the fear (giving a full description of the fear and its determinants as ascertained). An attempt has been made, in constructing the provisional list of headings, to avoid composite symptom headings as far as possible.

Symptoms: Referral

DISTURBANCES MANIFESTED ON THE BODY: Relating to: Sleep:
Broken and Restless

The referral letter described this symptom simply as difficulty in sleeping. This was amplified by the mother as meaning that he would not go to sleep at the proper time and would waken most nights several times. He was usually taken into the parents' bed, where he threshed about and kept his parents awake. At the beginning of treatment he slept in the same bedroom as the parents. This problem was dealt with in two ways, firstly by interpretation of Andy's fear that the mother might go away while he slept, his wish to separate the parents, and his wish to join their exciting intercourse; secondly by encouraging the mother to provide another bedroom for him and relieving her anxiety about him.

He moved into a bedroom of his own and after a few nights of broken sleep, he slept the whole night through from 6:30 P.M. to 6 A.M.—the first time since he was an infant. Thereafter the pattern varied from time to time. Sometimes he slept all night through, sometimes he awoke during the night. When he awoke, however, the sound of either parent's voice was sufficient to allow him to go back to sleep. During the last month or two prior to indexing his sleep has been sound and there appears to be no difficulty now. (Interview with mother and child [Chapter 3],

Interview with parents [Chapter 4], Weekly Reports Nos. 1, 2, 3, 4, 5, 28.)

(Second Indexing): There were no further sleep disturbances until the last few weeks in treatment, when, under the impact of termination, he frequently awoke during the night. He would go back to sleep again when the light was left on. This disturbance started to abate at the end of treatment and disappeared within a few weeks. An example of the joint handling by Andy and his mother of a situation which would formerly have given rise to difficulties was reported by the mother: he had been coughing through the night and could not sleep. She did not insist on his staying in his own bedroom, but made up a bed for him in the parental bedroom and he eventually went to sleep there. The following night, as his cough still seemed to be troublesome, she offered to repeat this, but Andy insisted on returning to his own bedroom, saying that his cough was better, and in fact he slept the whole night through. (Weekly Reports Nos. 42, 43, 49, 50.)

SYMPTOMS: Referral

DISTURBANCES MANIFESTED ON THE BODY: Relating to: Sleep: Falling Asleep, Difficulty in

Andy was said to have difficulty in going to sleep at what his mother considered the proper time. This was interpreted as his fear that his mummy might not be there if he woke up. At the same time the therapist suggested to the mother that the bedtime be not fixed for the time being, so as to shift the focus away from that aspect of the difficulty. The first response was that Andy slept all through each night after going to bed between 9 and 10:30 P.M. His bedtime gradually became earlier until at the end of seven months of treatment there was no difficulty about his going to sleep at an earlier hour. (Interview with mother and child [Chapter 3], Weekly Reports Nos. 1, 2, 28.)

SYMPTOMS: Referral

DISTURBANCES MANIFESTED ON THE BODY: Relating to: Sleep: Leaving Bed or Bedroom

Andy spent a large part of each night in the parents' bed, and this had been initiated by the mother. It had developed into a mutual arrangement, however, and on his side was seen and interpreted as his wish to separate the parents and to join them in exciting intercourse.

Following on the improvement of the sleeping symptoms and when a stage had been reached in which Andy remained in his own bedroom during the night, the father got a new job which involved his being away from home one night each week. His mother then used to leave her bedroom door open and when Andy wakened during the night he came into her bed. She was encouraged by the therapist to close her door and to get up and go to Andy if he should wake. His wish to take father's place in father's absence was interpreted and the leaving of the bedroom stopped.

He does not now awaken very often and when he does the mother goes to his room to comfort him, give him a drink, etc., and he soon falls asleep again. (Interview with parents [Chapter 4], Weekly Reports Nos. 1, 2, 21, 22, 23.)

SYMPTOMS: Referral

DISTURBANCES OF SOCIAL BEHAVIOR: Aggressiveness

At referral Andy was reported to be very aggressive to other children, with the exception of one friend. His facial expression was often observed to be pugnacious. His play was described as overactive and destructive, and his father reported that Andy had to be restrained from flinging things around at home as there was so much glass around.

Early in treatment his mother reported that he had bitten a a three-year-old boy cousin and that he had done this quite often. She also said that he has a game in his bath of biting the sponge and facecloth, shaking them as a puppy will. This was often observed in sessions with toys, and he also attempted to bite the therapist. Aggressiveness was also expressed verbally in the Clinic by his rude remarks to passers-by on the stairs, telling them that they stink and addressing them as "Mrs. Bum." Interpretation of the aggressiveness was that it derived from anger against mother (or therapist), e.g., when afraid of being left, but also as a wish to incorporate the object by biting to avoid separation. The immediate reaction was always an intensification of the aggressiveness, but the long-term response has been an almost complete disappearance of the symptom at home and to a large extent during sessions.

Another element underlying the aggressiveness was his expression of love in aggressive terms. (Interview with mother and child; Weekly Reports Nos. 2, 10, 16; "Incorporation" interpretation not recorded.)

SYMPTOMS: Referral

DISTURBANCES OF SOCIAL BEHAVIOR: Overexcitable

Andy's mother complained of his restlessness and overactive play, especially when with other children, and she feared that he would wear himself out. As an example of this she quoted his constant "quarreling" with a puppy. The overexcitability was often seen in treatment, in which an imaginative game would quickly become transformed into uncontrolled aggressiveness; he would throw things round the room and this would be accompanied by shouting and much body movement, and often culminated in a desire to urinate. Factors in the overexcitability which were understood and interpreted were his anal-sadistic intercourse fantasies, his exciting play with grandfather, displacement of aggression, and as being defensive against castration anxiety. (Interview with mother and child [Chapter 3], Weekly Reports Nos. 1, 2, 3, 4, 5, 7, 8.)

(Second Indexing): This symptom disappeared gradually in treatment and at home, but reappeared during sessions at a time when there was an upset between his parents about father's infidelity and there was a possible move of home being discussed. The link was interpreted in terms of his anxiety and uncertainty about adults staying in the same place. The restlessness disappeared within a day or two. (Weekly Report No. 36.)

SYMPTOMS: Emerged

DISTURBANCES MANIFESTED ON THE BODY: Relating to: Other Bodily Phenomena: Colds, Feverish

Mother reported that Andy has frequent colds, usually feverish, and she fears repetitions of convulsions at such times. Meaning not understood at time of indexing. (Reported by mother, not in reports.)

(Second Indexing): The frequency of these colds during treatment did not appear to be excessive to the therapist. That the mother reported it was seen, therefore, as part of her anxiety and concern, rather than as indicating a psychosomatic symptom in the child. (Weekly Report No. 48.)

SYMPTOMS: Emerged

DISTURBANCES OF SOCIAL BEHAVIOR: Provocative

Andy was observed to be provocative to his mother. He used certain swearwords frequently, e.g., "fuck" and "bleeding," at home, in public, and in sessions. His mother hated this and always scolded him for it. One day when the therapist said to her, in Andy's presence, that Andy disliked the idea of a baby coming, Andy picked up a toy calf and threw it away, saying, "Fuck the Pope." At one session, during which both parents were present, his father showed amusement at his swearing and his mother reported that he says "fuck" only during sessions now, not elsewhere. The provocative behavior was seen in the transference, e.g., in his delaying tactics on the stairs going up to the treatment room, and was understood as a means of inviting punishment so that his aggression will be controlled by an external agency, but also as part of his intercourse fantasies in which his being smacked is making a baby with the smacker. (Weekly Reports Nos. 2, 6.)

SYMPTOMS: Transitory

FEARS AND PHOBIAS: Animals

The term *Phobia* is used descriptively to cover avoidance behavior (expressed verbally or in action).

Andy's mother reported that he had become afraid of cats and dogs. This was closely associated with his playing at being an animal during sessions and the mechanisms involved were projection of his aggression onto the animals, identification with them, and control of the aggressive toy animals (i.e., his own aggression) by making them small and ordering them about.

Another element involved in this symptom was the previous displacement of his fear of father as retaliatory castrator to fantasy animals such as tigers and wolves. The fear of real cats and dogs disappeared and there was talk once more of Andy's acquiring a puppy. (Weekly Reports Nos. 3, 10, 11, 12, 23.)

CHAPTER 15

TREATMENT SITUATION AND TECHNIQUE

The subheadings in this section describe several aspects of the treatment situation and technique, viz.:

1. The patient's reaction to events inside and outside the session which affect the treatment (including acting out and transference, but not including dreams and fantasies, since these are indexed under separate headings);

2. Extrasessional contact of the therapist with the patient and with others for purposes of obtaining information, modifying the environment, etc.;

3. The aim of treatment, frequency of sessions and interruptions, and the reasons for terminating treatment;

4. Aspects of technique (e.g., interpretations, manipulation, management, etc.) and of the role of the therapist in the treatment situation.

TREATMENT SITUATION & TECHNIQUE: Activities & Behavior

ON COMING AND GOING

Under the heading *Activities and Behavior* are listed the child's occupations during the session (e.g., playing games, telling stories, etc.) as well as items referring to the child's attitudes and behavior (e.g., attacks on the therapist, the showing of affection, being messy or overanxious to please, etc.).

All activities and behavioral manifestations during the treatment session may express significant material. However, the therapist's emphasis on an understanding of certain aspects or more general attitudes and occupations of the child varies; children also vary in regard to the use of specific activities or behavioral manifestations for the expression of specific content.

One of the subheadings employed is *Means of Communication Used by Child*. The emphasis here is on the way the child brings material voluntarily or involuntarily. Under *General* we include *activities* which the patient prefers and typical behavioral manifestations through which he generally conveys his material (including resistances and acting out).

The general pattern was for Andy to start the session on the stairs with play and fantasies. He wanted to hold the therapist's hand. At one stage he crawled upstairs on hands and knees, asking to be carried. The crawling stopped when it was interpreted as his wish to be a little baby.

During the same period he had various methods of coming downstairs—on his knees, on his back, on his front. This behavior was provocative and was concurrent with provocative behavior at home. It invited smacking as a means of controlling his aggression and as part of his intercourse fantasies.

On leaving sessions he sometimes played a hiding and finding game, running away from the therapist to hide behind a coat hanging up on one of the landings. He screamed with delight on being found. This was seen as an acting out of the anticipated reunion with the therapist the following day, a means of controlling his anxiety about separating. When he met staff members on his way to and from the session, he was frequently aggressive toward them, calling them "Mrs. Bum" or "fuckie bogies." He often "shot" the males he met. When a certain point in his positive relationship with the therapist had been reached, he would hold his hand on going downstairs and then launch himself into space. (Weekly Reports Nos. 1, 5, 6, 7, 9, 10, 29, 31.)

TREATMENT SITUATION & TECHNIQUE: Activities & Behavior
DURING SESSION: Summary

Andy was usually very active, indeed often overactive, during sessions, played games with trains, dolls, bricks, and plasticine, moving furniture, jumping on and off couch and tables. Very often his excitement reached such a pitch that he would throw articles around the room or would suddenly want to urinate. He always accompanied his activities with either words or yelling.

Occasionally he would lie on the couch and invite the therapist to tell him a story and would be willing to tell a story in return.

At one stage he was destructive toward the fittings in the room and when he played with water in the sink, this invariably ended with his deliberately splashing water on the floor. This developed into direct aggression toward the therapist whom he would bite, occasionally kick, and often use as a target for various missiles ranging from plasticine to chair—he even attempted to lift the couch to throw. (Weekly Reports Nos. 1, 3, 4, 5, 15.)

(Second Indexing): In the last few months of treatment the destructiveness and direct aggression disappeared; he played building games or games with trains and figures which usually had a "story line," e.g., cowboys and Indians. He reverted for a time to washing games, but these were played without the former messiness. (Weekly Reports Nos. 41, 42, 44.)

TREATMENT SITUATION & TECHNIQUE: Activities & Behavior
DURING SESSIONS: Means of Communication Used by Child:
   General

Communication was by behavior, usually accompanied by verbalization of some aspect of the fantasies inherent in most of the activities. Throwing objects around the room or at the therapist was a favorite activity. There was no item which Andy could lift which he did not throw. Frequently the throwing was a displacement of anger to the articles thrown, but it was also a direct expression of rage. Sometimes, however, it was an exuberant and unrestrained expression of undirected aggressive impulses and he derived great pleasure from it.

Physical contact was much used in many varieties—hitting, kicking, biting, scratching, pinching, hugging, kissing, holding hands, sitting on the therapist's knee. These were direct expressions of love and hate, most often transference manifestations, but sometimes to the therapist as a friend or a frustrator. (Weekly Reports Nos. 1, 3, 8, 9, 12, 15, 22, 23.)

(Second Indexing): Except for occasional lapses into behavioral communication, especially at the beginning of the terminal phase of treatment, his communications became almost entirely verbal, especially those relating to his aggression. He was also able to ask direct questions about termination. (Weekly Reports Nos. 43, 44, 46.)

TREATMENT SITUATION & TECHNIQUE: Activities & Behavior

DURING SESSIONS: Means of Communication Used by Child: Specific

The subheading *Specific* includes specific actions or behavioral manifestations which have a definite meaning or which serve to express various content.

Andy repeatedly smacked a doll and a teddy bear, putting soap in his own mouth. He then put the doll on top of the teddy bear and when this was interpreted as his wish for the therapist and him to be together again, like mummy and daddy, he said, "Yes, he smacks her and he bites her."

Context: There had been a break in treatment due to the therapist's absence. Preceding themes had been his wish to make a baby with the therapist and his wish to clean (i.e., control his aggression).

Fantasy was understood as sadistic intercourse to celebrate reunion. That this was his concept of loving intercourse was shown by his immediate wish to sit on the therapist's knee and draw with him; but when his wish to have such intercourse (i.e., that the therapist should love him by smacking and biting) was interpreted, he started throwing pencils and tumblers to the floor. The tumbler smashed and he was very anxious.

TREATMENT SITUATION & TECHNIQUE: Activities & Behavior
DURING SESSIONS: Means of Communication Used by Child:
Specific

(a) Play with toy animals
Andy would put the animals on top of one another to give them
a ride and they inevitably fell off; he put them to bed and then
threw them out again. One animal, a horse, escaped this fate
and this animal represented himself, but also the father. This
play represented his parental intercourse fantasy and his aggressive response. (Weekly Report No. 1.)

(b) Urination during session time
He frequently wished to urinate during session time. At first
when he needed his mother to help him with his clothing, this
was a means of allaying his anxiety about her whereabouts. Later
it was a sequel to some exciting phallic fantasy, and still later
it was used as a resistance. (Weekly Reports Nos. 1, 23.)

(c) Water play
This consisted of his washing various toys, principally dolls which
represented babies or himself. The play invariably ended with
excited splashing and scooping water onto walls and floor and
had to be stopped. This restriction at first made him angry with
the therapist, but he was able to continue play by pretending
that the water was there. At one stage of treatment this was his
preferred activity and related to his identification with mother.
(Weekly Reports Nos. 7, 8, 9.)

TREATMENT SITUATION & TECHNIQUE: Contact with Parents

REASONS, ARRANGEMENTS, METHOD

Contact with parents for reasons of mother guidance, for
obtaining information, for assessing the home situation, etc.,
may be indexed here.

    The reason for the contact, the arrangements made, the
method of the approach adopted, and the child's reaction to
these in treatment should be indicated wherever possible.

Since Andy was only two years five months old at the beginning of treatment, his mother at first accompanied him to the sessions. She was an anxious young woman, very guilty about her ambivalence toward him, and unconsciously afraid of his being taken away from her. Communication by the therapist was accordingly directed at both mother and child during these early interviews. Father joined one of these sessions. When Andy was able to come to the sessions alone, his mother was seen at irregular intervals thereafter, but it soon became apparent that her disturbance was such as to demand regular interviews. It was also felt that this would insure her continued cooperation. She was therefore seen once a week alone. She chose to report on Andy's behavior at home, but frequently brought problems of her own. Interviews with her are included in the weekly reports.

It was hoped that the father would also be seen fairly frequently, but his work arrangements precluded this and he was seen only three times altogether. Interviews were often offered to him, but something always turned up to prevent his coming to see the therapist. (Interview with mother and child [Chapter 3], Weekly Reports Nos. 1, 5, 6, 8, 11.)

(Second Indexing): Because of a marital upset and its effect on the patient, more strenuous efforts were made to see the father more frequently, and eventually he came to see the therapist in alternate weeks. It was felt that some help and understanding in his problems would make the whole family situation easier and that this would be reflected in the parents' handling of Andy. Although there was no direct discussion of father's problems, he seemed to derive help from these sessions and he started to play more consistently with Andy. (Weekly Reports Nos. 35, 38, 40.)

TREATMENT SITUATION & TECHNIQUE

INTERPRETATIONS, REACTION TO

This section is primarily for cards describing general ways in which the child reacts to interpretations, e.g., by silences, by aggressive outbursts, by providing more material spontaneously, etc. The ways in which a child's reactions indicate the correctness or incorrectness of an interpretation would also be indexed here. If this habitual mode of reacting is understood as a transference phenomenon, a cross-reference should be made to *Transference*. Reactions to specific interpretations may be found under other headings in the index, unless the therapist particularly wishes to stress the reaction to such an interpretation, in which case it could be indexed here.

There are four main types of reaction to interpretation, viz.: (1) complete ignoring of the therapist; (2) repeated saying of "Eh?" *ad infinitum;* (3) repeated yelling of "Shut up"; (4) immediate agreement with the interpretation, usually accompanied by confirmatory material, in action, words, or both. Any of these reactions may be followed by behavioral changes. (Weekly Reports Nos. 1, 3, 4, 5, 7.)

(Second Indexing): To this list should be added the more mature response noted toward the end of treatment; viz., the interpretation of his ambivalence was met with resistance during the session, but outside the session it was obvious that it had been subjected to the processes of thought and that he was testing out the interpretation in relation to his mother. (Weekly Report No. 45.)

TREATMENT SITUATION & TECHNIQUE

INTERRUPTIONS, REACTIONS PRIOR TO

Any break in treatment occasioned by change of therapist, holidays, hospitalization, etc., is considered to be an interruption. An intended termination may become an interruption, e.g., in the case of a second therapist being found for a child when this was not thought possible immediately after the departure of the first therapist. Cards indexed under this heading should give the reasons for and the nature of the interruptions as well as the child's reaction to them and the meaning of the latter.

The only reaction prior to an interruption, which was seen and understood as such, occurred in the short interval between the resumption following an interruption occasioned by Andy having measles at the beginning of a holiday break. He displayed anxiety and a wish to cancel the holiday by telling the therapist each day that the therapist was *not* going on a holiday the next day. (Weekly Reports Nos. 18, 19.)

TREATMENT SITUATION & TECHNIQUE

INTERRUPTIONS, REACTION SUBSEQUENT TO

The first interruption early in treatment was occasioned by the Christmas holiday, and no apparent reaction was seen, the sessions continuing on resumption as if there had been no interruption.

The second interruption occurred at the end of February and beginning of March, and was due to a family emergency of the therapist. On resumption, Andy's anger was immediately apparent and was displaced to a doll which he scolded and smacked.

In the week following this resumption, another interruption occurred, as he contracted measles. On his return Andy told the therapist that he loved him and spoke of his fears that the therapist had died. He referred to the interruption as having been occasioned by the therapist's having a holiday. The next interruption was at Easter and once again he showed anger, but delayed until the second session after resumption. The therapist was ill very shortly after this and when treatment was resumed after a break of only a few days the material was not understood as being reactive to the interruption. (Weekly Reports Nos. 7, 14, 15, 16, 17, 18, 20, 21.)

TREATMENT SITUATION & TECHNIQUE

RELATIONSHIP TO THERAPIST

The therapist may index under this heading any information reflecting aspects of the child's relationship to the therapist which are felt by the therapist to refer to him as a person in his own right and are not considered to be primarily transference phenomena.

Andy frequently addresses the therapist as "friend," but a friend who can be sworn at and told when he is disliked; e.g., one day coming upstairs to his session he was angry with the therapist and followed him at a distance of a few yards. Every time the therapist looked round, Andy yelled "Shut up." Another staff member passing asked Andy whether he was telling *her* to shut up, to which he replied, "No, my *friend* is to shut up." (Weekly Report No. 9.)

TREATMENT SITUATION & TECHNIQUE: Transference

GENERAL CHARACTERISTICS

There was a marked readiness to use the therapist as a transference figure and this readiness was not confined to any particular dynamic sphere. At the same time the therapist was experienced as a real person easily distinguishable by the child from the therapist in his various transference roles.

TREATMENT SITUATION & TECHNIQUE: Transference

PHASES

The text of cards indexed under *Phases* should give a brief summary of the stages through which the transference passed during the course of treatment.

Throughout the early months of treatment there was a transference background, as it were, of aggression and aggressive play, derived from the relationship with the paternal grandfather, with whom aggressive and exciting play was a feature of Andy's home-life. Against this background more specific features of Andy's relationships with his parents were transferred.

At first the therapist was experienced in the transference as a parent—either parent, indiscriminately—who would act as partner in intercourse, to make babies with. Then the therapist's role became variously that of the mother as preoedipal love object; mother as oedipal love object, with father as rival (castrating and castrated); mother as the potential producer of baby rivals; and, for a short time only, father as the object of libidinal cathexis (a temporary negative oedipal love object).

In the last two months prior to indexing, both mother and father appeared in the transference as individual objects of aggression; they were seen as abandoners, and as such evoked anxiety and aggression, and this was experienced in the transference, concurrently with oedipal strivings and conflicts. (Weekly Reports Nos. 2, 3, 4, 5, 6, 7, 9, 10, 11, 12, 13, 15, 18, 19, 20, 21, 22, 23, 26.)

(Second Indexing): In the following phase the transference became obscured because there were difficulties between the parents which had repercussions on Andy, so that he was too concerned with the original objects for much to be transferred to the therapist, and earlier disturbances (e.g., about sleeping) were reactivated. When this phase was overcome, the therapist was at first seen as the critical parent. Andy dealt with this by turning passive into active and being critical of the therapist. On one occasion, after being very critical and, in turn, expecting criticism, he actually called the therapist "Mummy," immediately correcting himself by saying, "Aren't I a silly thing, I got you all mixed up, friend."

Following this the therapist was used as a substitute for an age peer, but it was unclear as to who this child was. During the terminal stages of treatment there was an interesting fluctuation in the transference manifestations. Reactive to his fear of being left he was negativistic and aggressive toward the therapist and clinging and demanding toward the mother. These attitudes toward the transference object soon disappeared, to be replaced by a gradual decathexis of the therapist. There was considerable lag, however, in any change in his behavior toward the mother. This was understood as a reactivation of old problems about separating due to termination and a return toward the original, still-present object (mother) away from the transference object. (Weekly Reports Nos. 35, 37, 41, 46.)

Treatment Situation & Technique: Transference

transferred features: Father, Mother's Partner

By *Transferred Features* is meant the *Transferred Features of Object Relationships or Life Situations.* Each card should give an example of the activities, behavior, verbalizations, etc., by which an aspect of the transference manifested itself as well as the meaning attributed to it.

On occasion when his mother was present during sessions Andy made so much noise as to make it impossible for therapist and

mother to communicate with each other. This was seen as a
transference of his wish to keep his parents apart. On one occasion, after insisting that his mother accompany him to the session, he shouted at the therapist whenever the latter or mother
tried to speak. He stood in the middle of the room, arms folded,
puffing through his nose, and yelling a stream of his swearwords
at the therapist. On the interpretation of his wish for mother and
therapist not to talk to each other, he suddenly lay down on the
couch and said that his daddy had gone to work to get his money,
daddy is going away on a boat, he didn't like daddy. This was
seen as a transference of his anxiety about father's hypothetical
departure, associated with the wish to separate mother and
father. (Weekly Reports Nos. 2, 7.)

TREATMENT SITUATION & TECHNIQUE: Transference

TRANSFERRED FEATURES: Father, (Negative) Oedipal Love
   Object

When his play one day showed identification with mother, the
therapist interpreted this and Andy immediately laid himself
down on the couch, drew up his legs, opened them, and put his
hand on his penis. This was interpreted as his playing at what
mummy does in bed with daddy and that he wanted the therapist to do it to him. He denied this and asked for the therapist's
keys to open his locker. He tried for only a few seconds to open
it, then gave up. He clutched at his penis and said, "Oh me little
winkie." This was interpreted as his wish to be the mummy to
me as daddy, but his fear that this would mean the loss of his
penis. He said that the bleeding tiger would cut it off, but he
would not let it. (Weekly Report No. 12.)

TREATMENT SITUATION & TECHNIQUE: Transference

TRANSFERRED FEATURES: Father, Wish to Castrate Father, and
   Fear of Being Castrated by Father

In the oedipal situation father was seen in various guises as a
threatening person. His fear of father as a castrator was closely
related to his wish to castrate father. One day when the therapist
asked him to tell a story in return for one the therapist had told
him, he said that once upon a time a little boy met a gee-gee and

the gee-gee bit the little boy and the boy said fuck and told the gee-gee get out. Having told this story he stood up and held his penis, saying he would put a pin in his winkie, then changed this to saying that he would put a pin in the therapist's winkie. Then followed several days on which he dawdled on the way upstairs to treatment, being conciliatory and not directly aggressive during sessions and finally very provocative after sessions. (Weekly Reports Nos. 3, 4, 6.)

TREATMENT SITUATION & TECHNIQUE: Transference

TRANSFERRED FEATURES: Father, Who May Leave Him

When his father started a new job which entailed his absence from home one night each week, Andy was markedly negative toward the therapist, particularly on Fridays, and often told the therapist to shut up, that he did not like him. This was seen as anger at the father's absence transferred to the therapist. (Weekly Reports Nos. 23, 26).

TREATMENT SITUATION & TECHNIQUE: Transference

TRANSFERRED FEATURES: Mother, Oedipal Love Object

When fantasies of making a baby with the therapist were interpreted as Andy's wish to make a baby with mummy, associations were produced indicating his fear of castration—monkeys would throw rocks at him, try to hit him on the belly, hit him on the winkie.

On another occasion he played at going to bed on the couch, asking for a cup of tea, then orange, then Ribena. When the therapist commented that Andy was playing at doing what he does with mummy before he goes to sleep in his real bed, Andy replied, "Yes, good night, come on, come and lie down beside me." The therapist added that Andy wanted to play at doing what mummy and daddy do when they go to bed, and Andy responded with a very good-natured smile and the endearment, said very lovingly, "You fuckie bogie." (Weekly Reports Nos. 9, 12, 15, 21, 23.)

TREATMENT SITUATION & TECHNIQUE: Transference

TRANSFERRED FEATURES: Mother, Potential Producer of Baby Rivals

Following a break in treatment, Andy would not come to the treatment room with his mother. She reported that he had missed the therapist and had asked whether the therapist was with anybody. When his mother left the room he cried. When the therapist verbalized Andy's anger at the break, he asked who the therapist had been with, adding, "I thought you was with another friend." The therapist defined this other friend as another little boy, and Andy became furious and threw practically everything in the room at the therapist. (Weekly Report No. 15).

TREATMENT SITUATION & TECHNIQUE: Transference

TRANSFERRED FEATURES: Mother, Satisfier of Early Needs

Several features of this relationship were transferred to the therapist, notably the oral dependence. At one stage Andy would crawl upstairs and ask to be carried by the therapist. He sometimes asked to sit on the therapist's knee. After the Easter break (further extended because of the therapist's illness) he played with plasticine animals, giving them pieces of plasticine much bigger than themselves, saying, "Poor pussy [dog, moo-cow, etc.] is hungry—he hasn't had anything to eat for a long time." This was interpreted as his feeling of not being fed by the therapist, related to earlier feelings of not getting enough from mummy. The verbal response was "Well, she's got me now" and telling the therapist to shut up; the nonverbal response was to throw the plasticine at the wall. (Weekly Reports Nos. 6, 12, 20.)

TREATMENT SITUATION & TECHNIQUE: Transference

TRANSFERRED FEATURES: Mother, Who May Leave Him

Aggression toward the mother as someone who abandoned or may abandon Andy was transferred to the therapist at times of separation. Following a short period of absence on account of his illness, Andy had difficulty in separating from his mother in the waiting room, and during sessions he played at moving house and throwing things about the room. He was careful not to hit the therapist with anything, but accompanied the activity with many oaths and declarations of his dislike of the therapist. Although the absence had been caused by Andy's illness, he spoke of the therapist's having been on holiday and referred to the impending Easter holiday at each session by saying, "You're not going on holiday tomorrow." (Weekly Reports Nos. 19, 22.)

TREATMENT SITUATION & TECHNIQUE: Transference

TRANSFERRED FEATURES: Parent, Partner in Making Babies

At one stage Andy transferred his wish to have either parent as his partner in intercourse, to make babies with. It seemed to be immaterial which parent took this role. He played many games in which motor cars and animals were crashed together and he invited the therapist to join these games. On one occasion, having crashed two cars together, he put them in the wastepaper basket. The therapist interpreted Andy's wish that they should make a baby together and that Andy thought babies are made like jobbies, whereupon Andy rattled the cars about in the basket, incanted "Fuckie bogie" over it, then sat on the basket and grinned. Fluctuation in his taking both active and passive roles in baby-making was shown when he smacked a moo-cow, then put a baby moo-cow beside it, saying, "There's a sister baby now" and then put the baby in the wastepaper basket. He turned to the therapist and, with a wheedling smile, said, "You do it to me now." (Weekly Reports Nos. 5, 6, 7, 9.)

TREATMENT SITUATION & TECHNIQUE: Technique

TERMINATION OF TREATMENT: Handling of

The decision was made by the supervisor and therapist that treatment should terminate, in its intensive form, after fourteen months, particularly if the child continued to show signs of readiness for nursery school. As these signs were forthcoming, termination was discussed with the mother. The mistake was made of not speaking to Andy immediately about it. When it became apparent that his mother had done so, it was then taken up with him. The approach made by the therapist was that Andy had been coming to see him every day because there had been things which had been making the child unhappy, but now that he was so much happier, he would not need to come to see the therapist so often, but would come one day every week after Christmas.

The content of termination material was very much concerned with his problem of being left, and was dealt with by interpretation of the transference. (Weekly Reports Nos. 41, 43-50.)

TREATMENT SITUATION & TECHNIQUE: Technique

TERMINATION: Reasons for

Termination was decided on because of the symptomatic improvement and his firm establishment in the oedipal phase. Bearing in mind the strength of his progressive tendency, analysis was regarded as having been sufficiently successful to enable him to function well in the nursery school situation, i.e., to move out of the closed family situation.

TREATMENT SITUATION & TECHNIQUE: Technique

TERMINATION: Reaction to Impending Termination

(Second Indexing): Termination had been discussed with the mother before it was broached with Andy. When he went back to the aggressive delaying in coming to sessions which had been a feature of the early stages of treatment, it became obvious that his mother had spoken about termination either to him or in his presence, and that the negativism was a reaction to the impending termination. The therapist immediately took this up with Andy and he confirmed that feelings about termination had provoked the delaying behavior by telling the therapist that he did not like him and asking why he could not come to play with the therapist every day. (Weekly Report No. 43.)

TREATMENT SITUATION & TECHNIQUE: Technique

INTERVENTION, NONVERBAL: Permission to Take Things Home

Intervention (by many analysts now called manipulation or management) refers to any deliberate activity that is not an interpretation but is used by the therapist for the purposes of treatment. The reason for the intervention, the methods adopted, and the expected outcome should be given. A distinction is made between nonverbal and verbal interventions.

When playing with teddy bears and dolls during sessions Andy often wanted to take some of them home with him. The therapist felt that frustration of such wishes in such a young child was unnecessary in the interests of treatment, and also hoped that his mother would report on his play with these toys at home. She reported that one teddy bear became his bedmate for several weeks, but that the others were apparently ignored at home, although he would often refuse to have them returned. (Weekly Reports Nos. 7, 13; Mother's statement, not in reports.)

TREATMENT SITUATION & TECHNIQUE: Technique

INTERVENTION, NONVERBAL: Physical Contact and Restraint

Physical contact of many kinds was sought by Andy, e.g., hitting, kicking, holding hands, sitting on the therapist's knee, etc. On the whole, a permissive attitude was adopted by the therapist toward such contacts. The reasons for such permissiveness were, in the beginning, to establish the treatment relationship on the basis of the therapist's being a friend (and therefore not too unlike parents and grandparents) and a safe person. Limitations were put on contacts, however, to the extent of not letting Andy actually hurt the therapist and interpreting the wish to hurt, together with the assurance that the therapist would not allow himself to be really hurt. Similarly, wishes to be carried and so on were interpreted variously as Andy's wish to be treated as a baby and as his wish to show how much he loved the therapist (as real object as well as transference object). Aggressive contacts came to be sought less and less as Andy verbalized his aggression more. Similarly, loving contacts became associated less with body contact and were seen more in his attitude toward the therapist. (Weekly Reports Nos. 1, 8, 9, 12, 22, 23, 24, 25.)

TREATMENT SITUATION & TECHNIQUE: Technique

INTERVENTION, NONVERBAL: Physical Restraint

Andy had to be restrained on several occasions, particularly when he used to pull at the towel rail (which he finally managed to pull away from the wall) and the not very well fixed wash basin; also at the climax of his washing games when he would splash water all over the place. Verbal comment by the therapist was usually along the lines that the therapist would not allow Andy to hurt him or to cause too much damage. Restraint varied from lifting him bodily away from the object he was attacking to pulling out the plug and tightening the taps. Responses were invariably fury at the therapist and sometimes retaliatory physical attack. (Weekly Reports Nos. 4, 8, 9.)

TREATMENT SITUATION & TECHNIQUE: Technique
INTERVENTION, NONVERBAL: Presents

The therapist gave Andy an Easter gift of a cardboard train filled with small eggs, following broad hints that a gift was expected. The therapist felt that not to give a present would be to frustrate Andy unnecessarily and that he would be unable to understand the reasons for not giving him one. However, when his birthday came, no present was given, although one was held in reserve. There was a great struggle within Andy to accept the fact that one can be liked without tangible proof having to be given. He expected another "eggie train" and was disappointed and angry when it did not appear. The disappointment was associated with being kept waiting by his parents for their birthday present to him. (Weekly Reports Nos. 25, 26.)

TREATMENT SITUATION & TECHNIQUE: Technique
MEANS OF COMMUNICATION USED BY THERAPIST: Stories

When interpretations, explanations or clarifications of material are made in any other than a direct verbal manner referring to the child himself, the method used may be indicated under this heading. Thus the vehicle for communicating both interpretations and precursors to interpretations may be indexed here (e.g., stories, games, etc.). The reason for the use of the method should be given.

Only in the first weeks were stories told by the therapist as a means of communication and then usually as follow-ups of stories told by Andy. The therapist's stories were barely disguised interventions; e.g., the therapist told him of a little boy who used to be frightened during the night, but when he knew him mummy was very near his bedroom if he wanted her, he was not frightened any more. (Weekly Report No. 4.)

TREATMENT SITUATION & TECHNIQUE: Technique

MEANS OF COMMUNICATION USED BY THERAPIST: Via Substitute Object: Puppets, etc.

Animals, dolls, teddy bear, puppets have all been used by the therapist to communicate with the patient along the lines that they are "like" Andy, mummy, daddy, etc., and have wishes, fears, and so on like his own; e.g., the gee-gee with which he was identified was used in this way. Another example was when he was playing with a doll aggressively, saying that he was biting her belly off. The therapist said that Andy thought the lady had a baby inside her, just like Auntie M. (who *was* pregnant), and he responded by saying furiously "Fuck it" and throwing the doll away. (Weekly Reports Nos. 1, 3.)

TREATMENT SITUATION & TECHNIQUE: Technique

TERMINATION: Stages in

(Second Indexing): Intensive treatment ceased after fourteen months. He was seen once weekly for a further four months. The plan was that he should then be seen at fortnightly intervals for a few months thereafter, but it became obvious that he had withdrawn cathexis to a degree in which he was almost completely uninterested in the interviews, so the interval between interviews was increased to a month.

TREATMENT SITUATION & TECHNIQUE: Technique

SPECIFIC METHOD: For a Toddler

When the therapist wishes to emphasize that a technique has been adopted in order to cope with specific problems or with a specific type of child, the problem (or the type of child) may be indexed under this heading.

It had been accepted by the therapist that there would be no question of having sessions alone with the patient at first, but that the mother (and possibly the father also) would be present to begin with. The technique devised was for the mother and therapist to sit facing each other across the table and for the child to be free to move around. The toy locker was opened at the beginning of each session and it contained a selection of articles which the therapist thought appropriate, e.g., wooden trains, motor cars, aeroplanes, animals, plasticine, miniature dolls, toy telephone, peg-hammering board.

To help the mother by guidance was an aim additional to the analytic aim with the child, so efforts were made to phrase interpretations and interventions so that they could be understood by both, as far as possible. These were usually overtly directed at the mother, but occasionally an interpretation intended for the mother was directed at the child. After the first two weeks the mother stopped coming into the sessions every day of her own accord, but during the treatment there have been occasions when the child insisted on her coming with him to the treatment room. No objection has ever been made to this by the therapist and a similar technique to that mentioned above was used on these occasions. (Weekly Reports Nos. 1, 2, 3.)

Treatment Situation & Technique: Technique

USE MADE OF EXTRA-ANALYTIC MATERIAL

This heading provides for the indexing of any instance in which material obtained from some source other than the child is used by the therapist for the purpose of treatment. Cards should describe the source of the information, the use of it, and the reasons for using it.

Information derived from the mother was freely used by the therapist in making interpretations and interventions arising from material supplied by the child, i.e., such information acted as confirmatory evidence and was not used unless supported by direct evidence from the child; for example, the therapist knew from the parents that Andy left his own bed to come into their bed during the night. At a session in which he played with a horse (with which the therapist knew Andy was identified), making a fence round it and then announcing that the horse was going to jump out, the therapist interpreted the horse's jumping out as being like Andy's wish to get out of bed to be with his parents, as the horse likes to be with the other moo-cows (animals). (Weekly Report No. 1.)

REFERENCES

Freud, A. (1965), *Normality and Pathology in Childhood.* New York: International Universities Press.

Joffe, W. G. & Sandler, J. (1965), Notes on Pain, Depression and Individuation. *The Psychoanalytic Study of the Child,* 20 (in press). New York: International Universities Press.

Sandler, J. (1960), On the Concept of Superego. *The Psychoanalytic Study of the Child,* 15:128-162. New York: International Universities Press.

——— (1962a), Psychology and Psychoanalysis. *Brit. J. Med. Psychol.,* 35:91.

——— (1962b), The Hampstead Index as an Instrument of Psycho-Analytic Research. *Int. J. Psycho-Anal.,* 43:287-291.

——— Holder, A. & Meers, D. (1963), The Ego Ideal and the Ideal Self. *The Psychoanalytic Study of the Child,* 18:139-158. New York: International Universities Press.

——— & Joffe, W. G. (1964a), Hobby, Skill and Sublimation. Paper presented at the Mid-Winter Meeting of the American Psychoanalytic Association, December, 1964.

——— ——— (1964b), The Depressive Response in Children. Paper presented at the Mid-Winter Meeting of the American Psychoanalytic Association, December, 1964.

——— ——— (1965), Notes on Obsessional Manifestations in Children. *The Psychoanalytic Study of the Child,* 20 (in press). New York: International Universities Press.

——— Kawenoka, M., Neurath, L., Rosenblatt, B., Schnurmann, A., & Sigal, J. (1962), The Classification of Superego Material in the Hampstead Index. *The Psychoanalytic Study of the Child,* 17:107-127. New York: International Universities Press.

——— & Nagera, H. (1963), Aspects of the Metapsychology of Fantasy. *The Psychoanalytic Study of the Child,* 18:159-194. New York: International Universities Press.

——— & Rosenblatt, B. (1962), The Concept of the Representational Word. *The Psychoanalytic Study of the Child,* 17:128-145. New York: International Universities Press.

ABOUT THE AUTHORS

JOHN BOLLAND, M.B., Ch.B., is Medical Director of The Hampstead Child-Therapy Clinic.

JOSEPH SANDLER, M.A., Ph.D., D.Sc., is Chairman of the Index Project, The Hampstead Child-Therapy Clinic, and Senior Lecturer in Psychopathology, The Middlesex Hospital Medical School.